First Published - 2009

ISBN: 978-81-907891-0-3

Published by

MADHAV BOOKS
F-2562, Palam Vihar
Gurgaon-122 017 (Haryana)
Phone : 0124-2365193, 9810373248

DEDICATED

To

MY RESPECTED PARENTS–

M. ABDUL HAMID

And

HOSNEARA BEGUM

CONTENTS

	Preface	ix
	Abbreviations	xiii
1.	Introduction to Human Rights of the Accused	1
2.	Constitutional Guarantees of the Accused	17
3.	Accused Persons and the Role of Police	61
4.	Right to Reasonable Investigation Process in Criminal Justice	100
5.	Right to a Fair Trial and the Prisoners Rights	122
6.	Interviews with the Accused and Different Officials	166
7.	General Conclusions	176
	Appendices	184
	Bibliography	198
	Index	209

PREFACE

Every criminal justice system has the obligation to protect human rights of the accused, because an accused is treated as innocent before conviction under the provision of law. The right to life, liberty and fair trial are the fundamental human rights of the accused. There is a genuine link between peace and human rights. This pursuit and preservation of peace and the security of humankind, the first stated purpose of the United Nations, necessitate the protection and implementation of human rights, without which human rights cannot be effectively achieved.

Infringement of the fundamental human rights to life, liberty, personal security and physical integrity affect individual rights as well as it has a negative impact on the equality of life. These infringements are a product of both state parties and politics involving national criminal processes when carried out under the colour of law by public officials. The topic 'human rights of the accused' is of universal concern that cuts across major legal and political boundaries. However, this study seeks to correlate internationally and nationally protected human rights, which are applicable in the criminal process. Human rights and constitutional guarantees of the accused; rights of arrested and detained persons with reference to the state of preventive detention under the Special Powers Act, 1974 and the role of police in Bangladesh; right to reasonable investigation, questioning, search and seizure; the right to a fair trial and the rights of prisoners in Bangladesh are set forth in details in this study and a comparison is made basically with the provisions in the Universal Declaration of Human Rights (UDHR) and the International Covenant on Civil and Political Rights (ICCPR).

Admittedly, this study is unique because it makes a comparison of international law and national criminal justice system. A comparison of the criminal jurisprudential philosophy in both international law and laws of Bangladesh should enable readers to distinguish the direction of human rights strategy being followed in both administration of criminal justice.

This book is actually the revised version of my PhD thesis entitled ***Human Rights of the Accused Under International Law and Municipal Law: A Case Study in Bangladesh (1990-2000)*** completed in 2005 in the Department of Law & Justice under the Faculty of Law of Rajshahi University, Bangladesh.

At the very first, I would like to express my earnest respect and thankfulness to Professor Dr. Begum Asma Siddiqua, Dean, Faculty of Law, Rajshahi University for her continued supervision, invaluable advice and direction that encouraged me immensely for putting my best endeavour throughout the work of the thesis. I also extend my sincere gratitude to Professor Dr. M. Faiz-ud-Din, Department of Law & Justice, Rajshahi University for sparing me his brilliant guidance in this study.

I would also like to acknowledge my deepest gratitude and gratefulness to my departmental colleagues for their continued support, especially my honourable teacher Dr. Sarkar Ali Akkas whose constant assistance I received throughout my studies.

I would also like to take opportunity to express my sincere thanks to Professor M. Shamsur Rahman, Department of Botany, Rajshahi University for providing me his valuable suggestions in the midst of his professional business. I am also grateful to my parents and other family members for giving me the strength to fight against all odds and complete this work successfully. I cannot conclude without thanking my wife

Mrs. Farhana Anzum for giving me her nice company during the crucial days of my studies.

Last, but not the least, I do record my heartiest indebtedness to the Intellectual Advancement Award (IAA), London and the Islami Bank Foundation, Bangladesh for their financial assistance to collect relevant data for the PhD thesis.

I hope and trust that this book will prove more responsive to the needs of the law students, academics, practicing lawyers, judges, member of the law enforcing agencies and policy makers than it has done ever before.

Any suggestion for the improvement of the book will be received with thanks. I shall consider my labour amply rewarded if the persons concerned find the book helpful and useful.

July, 2008

M ABDUL HANNAN
Associate Professor
Department of Law & Justice
Rajshahi University
Rajshahi 6205
BANGLADESH.

ABBREVIATIONS

ACHR	:	American Convention on Human Rights.
ADM	:	Additional District Magistrate.
AED	:	Academy for Educational Development.
AIR	:	All India Reporter (series).
AJIL	:	American Journal of International Law.
ASK	:	Ain O' Shalish Kendra.
BDR	:	Bangladesh Rifles.
BHRB	:	Bangladesh Human Rights Bureau.
BLAST	:	Bangladesh Legal Aid and Services Trust.
BMSP	:	Bangladesh Manobadhikar Shamannoy Parishad.
BNP	:	Bangladesh Nationalist Party.
BPF	:	Bangladesh Police Form.
BRCT	:	Bangladesh Rehabilitation Centre for Trauma Victims.
CAT	:	Convention against Torture and Other Cruel, Inhuman or Degrading Treatment or Punishment.
CEDAW	:	Convention on the Elimination of All Forms of Discrimination Against Women.
CMCH	:	Chittagong Medical College Hospital.
CMM	:	Chief Metropolitan Magistrate.

CrL J	:	Criminal Law Journal (series).
CrPC	:	Code of Criminal Procedure.
CWN	:	Calcutta Weekly Notes.
DIG	:	Deputy Inspector General.
DLR	:	Dhaka Law Reports (series).
DM	:	District Magistrate.
DP	:	Draft Principles on Freedom from Arbitrary Arrest and Detention.
ECHR	:	European Convention on Human Rights (Convention for the Protection of Human Rights and Fundamental Freedoms).
FIR	:	First Information Reports.
HCD	:	High Court Division.
HRC	:	Human Rights Committee.
IACHR	:	Inter-American Convention on Human Rights.
ICCPR	:	International Covenant on Civil and Political Rights.
ICJ	:	International Court of Justice.
IJIL	:	Indian Journal of International Law.
ILR	:	Indian Law Reports.
JRC	:	Jail Reforms Commission.
LEA	:	Law Enforcing Agencies.
LRM	:	Legal Remembrance Manual.
MLR	:	Main Stream Law Reports (series).
NHRC	:	National Human Rights Commission.
NHRI	:	National Human Rights Institute.
OC	:	Officer-in-charge.
PRB	:	Police Regulations of Bengal.
PRC	:	Prison Reform Committee.
PS	:	Police Station.
RAB	:	Rapid Action Battalions.

SCC	:	Supreme Court Cases.
SCR	:	Supreme Court Reports.
SPA	:	Special Powers Act.
TB	:	Tuberculosis.
UDHR	:	Universal Declaration of Human Rights.
UN	:	United Nations.
UNDP	:	United Nations Development Programme.
UNTS	:	United Nations Treaty Series.
URL	:	Uniform Resource Locator.

INTRODUCTION TO HUMAN RIGHTS OF THE ACCUSED 1

INTRODUCTION

Human rights are inherent in our nature and without these, the concept of society in which human beings live is meaningless.[1] These rights, irrespective of civil, political, social, economic or cultural rights and issues are inter-dependable as well as inter-linked. The absence of human rights in any society is basically a denial of human dignity.[2] Protection of human rights depends mainly on criminal justice system. Criminal justice is based on different stages of the court proceedings, functions of police and prosecutions such as filing of a case, arrest, investigation, framing of charge, trial, conviction or acquittal etc.

Human behaviour is a complicated phenomenon and irrational behaviour is due to unbalanced socio-economic, cultural and political conditions of the country, which result in committing crimes by the people. So, crimes are inevitably general feature of every society. The criminal law of every country defines certain acts, which it regards as crime and provides sanctions against individual who is held responsible for the commission of such acts. An individual who is charged with the commission of a crime is regarded as an accused. The right to defence enables the accused to defend him/her against the charges brought against him/her using all the facilities established by law. The accused can defend him/herself or with the help of a lawyer.[3]

The efforts for the protection of the rights of public in general and of the accused in particular have been addressed in many international human rights documents like the Universal Declaration of Human Rights, 1948,[4] the International Covenant on Civil and Political Rights, 1966,[5] the United Nations Standard Minimum Rules for the Treatment of Prisoners, 1957, the United Nations Draft Body of Principles for the Protection of All Persons under Any Form of Detention or Imprisonment, 1988 and in various domestic legislations. However, problems like delay in trials due to paucity of courts or judges and unhygienic environment in the jail caused by over-crowding of prisoners need to be examined for the protection of the rights of the accused. Protection of the rights and interests of the accused as well as their psychological and economic assistance is vitally important for the fair implementation of criminal laws and also for gaining public confidence in criminal justice system. Therefore, an exploration of those factors, which impair the criminal justice system and hinder the rights of the accused, are essentially important for the protection of the rights of the accused.

Literature related to the administration of criminal justice reveals that the concept of human rights of the accused has gradually been changing and developing over a period of time. The UDHR has accorded a new meaning to the human rights strategy in administration of criminal justice. New vistas were opened for the defence of accused and the promotion of their rights has been recognised as the legitimate objective of the international and national communities. The UDHR provides guiding principles for all countries and also normally from their criminal justice system in accordance with the international human rights laws for providing fair and just trial to the accused. The UDHR and the Covenant contain norms representing universal standards of conduct for all peoples and all nations. The guiding principles of the UDHR as well as of the ICCPR have been recognised and incorporated by almost all mature legal systems of the world. The framework of the International Covenant on Human Rights incorporates all aspects of religious, cultural or ideological backgrounds and provides a standard for different countries of the world. The General Assembly of the United Nations (UN) has emphasised that no state can claim to be allowed to disregard basic human rights such as the right to life, safeguard from torture and right to a fair trial. A departure from these standards might be permitted under the national or religious laws of a country under special circumstances.[6]

The quest for human rights has become a fundamental aim of the modern states. The twenty first century has witnessed the efforts of international community to develop national, regional and international measures for the protection and promotion of human rights. The purpose of this study is to show and examine the legal position of the accused and recognition of his/her rights within the sphere of international as well as municipal law of Bangladesh. The study will also reflect on human rights situation with regard to the accused in Bangladesh.

CRIMINAL ADMINISTRATION OF JUSTICE

Thomas Hobbs in his famous work *Laviathan* says "Man is by nature a fighting animal so it is inevitable to keep man in awe not of kings alone but of all mankind".[7] For that a sanction is very much necessary. When in a society there remains no sanction or a common power to keep them all in awe civilization become unattainable, unchecked injustice continues, the society could be said to be at war where all citizens were inimical with each other. There life becomes very insecured, danger of death exists, and it becomes poor, brutish and short. So men felt the necessity of force to be applied by the state. The main object behind this was to protect the society by punishing the criminals. For that the force became the exclusive instrument of justice. The society of private vengeancy had transmitted into criminal administration of justice in a modern society where state took over the function of punishing the wrongdoer and the evils. States moderated the force and applied the force by an institution namely the police. Because without institutionalised law enforcement man tend to redress his wrong by his own hands. But force as an instrument for the upheaval of mankind is nearly a temporal and provisional incident in the development of perfect civilization. In most of the societies of today force remain as latent as an element of administration of justice and declaration of rights and duties of the state on one hand and the declaring of the rights and duties of the subject on the other hand is enough for the state rather than the declaration of enforcement by way of force.[8] In order to ensure justice all these were done by the social thinkers. But it should also be brought into mind that merely punishing the evil alone does not ensure social justice. Justice requires that no one can be convicted without fair trial and it does not only mean that justice has been done but also it requires that justice should manifestly be seen to have been done.

Justice again requires that the offender or the accused as a member of the society should not be treated as an isolated island above the sea level, justice should be such that it does not bring any injustice for the offenders also. Justice should mean that the existing laws and the procedures of the application should not be detrimental to justice.

CRIME SITUATION IN BANGLADESH

In consideration of the provisions of the municipal law as recognised in the Constitution of Bangladesh and the statutory law, it is somewhat necessary to mention that the laws relating to the rights of the accused in Bangladesh, India and Pakistan are similar to a great extent. Every citizen of all the countries is governed by the law of the land as well as by his/her personal law. In the Constitution of Bangladesh various provisions regarding the protection of human rights have been incorporated under Part II and III namely, fundamental principles of state policy and fundamental rights either explicitly or implicitly. The violation of some of these rights may be considered as crime, e.g., violation of right to life, right to protection against torture, right to a fair trial etc.

These crimes may be committed either by private individual or by the Law Enforcing Agencies (LEA) like Police, Bangladesh Rifles (BDR) and ANSAR. The number of crimes committed by the LEA is increasing enormously in recent years and these are threatening the security of the people's life and property. Unfair exercise of third degree method[9] by police while questioning in the name of remand, malpractice of Sections 54 and 167 of the Code of Criminal Procedure, 1898[10] severely curtail the rights of the accused. Under the circumstances, it is necessary to discover the causes of violation of human rights of the accused, so that some possible measures could be taken for the promotion and protection of the rights of the accused.

In order to control crimes, wide powers are conferred by the statute upon the state to invoke the criminal justice system against the wrongdoers. But regards have to be paid upon the basic rights of wrongdoers and while conceding coercive powers of the state, it is to be seen that the state do not use arbitrary and capricious powers against the wrongdoers.[11] So every mature legal system of the world, whether be it the American, British, Indian or the Bangladeshi, treats the accused as innocent until and unless he/she is proved guilty beyond all reasonable doubts. This view has been expressed directly in the International Covenant that, "everyone charged with a criminal offence shall have the right to be presumed innocent until proved guilty according to law".[12]

The laws of Bangladesh are consistent with the norms and standards as adopted by the United Nations for the protection of the rights of the accused. The right to personal liberty of an individual is one of the most important basic human rights recognised in the UDHR.[13] It has also received a prominent place in the Covenant.[14] Similarly the Constitution of Bangladesh recognises it as a fundamental right in Article 32, which provides, "No person shall be deprived of life or personal liberty save in accordance with law". Right to life is an inherent right of a man and therefore, no man can take away the life of other man capriciously. This right has been guaranteed by all national and international laws.

The Constitution of Bangladesh solemnly pledges guarantee of fundamental rights to every citizen of the Republic. The Constitution has a separate chapter entitled

'Fundamental Rights' which comprises provisions regarding basic human rights in Articles 27 to 44.[15] The Preamble of the Constitution states " ...fundamental human rights and freedom, equality and justice, political, economic and social rights will be secured for all citizen". Article 11 of the Constitution states, "the Republic shall be a democracy in which fundamental human rights and freedom, and respect for the dignity and worth of the human person shall be guaranteed". Article 26(1) states that all laws inconsistent with fundamental human rights will be void.

ROLE OF THE GOVERNMENT IN CONTROLLING CRIME

The Constitution of Bangladesh upholds human rights, which came into force on 16 December 1972. After nine months of the date of the constitution becoming effective on 20 September1973, the Government had brought the Second Amendment to the Constitution pertaining to the provisions of the fundamental rights and used the Parliament to make repressive laws regarding arrest and detention. The original Constitution did not provide for proclamation of emergency and supervision of fundamental rights during emergency and in view of Article 33 of the original Constitution preventive detention was not possible. But by the second constitutional amendment the provision for preventive detention was imported and in part IX A of the Constitution power was conferred upon the Parliament and executive to deal with the emergency situation and suspension of rights, which are fundamental. Actual scheme of this amendment was not unjustified but its practice paved its ineffectiveness.[16] On 9 February 1974, the Government passed an oppressive law named, the Special Powers Act 1974,[17] which came as a stunning blow on political leaders, labour union activists, and the press. Almost all the time to date this law is being used politically by the Government for arresting and detaining their opponents.

In recent years there are broad range of violation of human rights by the Government and private groups. Many incidents of such violation are sources of worry and concern. Torture and death in police and jail custody show the trends of crimes against humanity are increasing gradually. Daily Newspaper reports on individual human rights violation and human rights abuse have become nation-wide phenomena. Violations of human rights by police, jail authorities and individual criminals in Bangladesh have become a daily affair. Life and property have become insecure both in and out of home. One study shows that, children and women are the victims to torture and acid throwing for which no effective measures have been taken.[18]

OBJECTIVES OF THE STUDY

This study is an attempt to make an evaluation of the procedural guarantees as accorded to the accused under international law and laws of Bangladesh. Considering the vastness of the area of administration of criminal justice this study focuses only on the rights of the accused at pre-trial and trial stages. In view of the studies the goal is reformulated into some specific objectives.

They are as follows:

- To identify the grounds of violation of the rights of the accused;
- To focus on the ways of making the current laws effective by mentioning their success and failure;
- To develop social awareness about the rights of the accused;
- To promote effectiveness of the authority for establishing human rights and to accelerate the dynamism in playing effective role of the authority by portraying the gross violation of human rights; and
- To find out ways and means of taking effective measures for establishing the rights of the accused.

In order to procure these objectives some sorts of standards are necessary to evaluate the conditions of human rights situation in Bangladesh. With this end in mind, the study aims at scrutinising general principles of law, policies, norms, mechanisms and practices concerning human rights of the accused. In this regard, the study reviews and analyses the secondary literature, international standards, law and practices of Bangladesh and of some other jurisdictions in accordance with the methodology of the study and the ways of treatment of the data discussed in sections 1.6 and 1.7.

METHODOLOGY OF THE STUDY

This study examines the law and practice relating to the rights of the accused both in international and Bangladesh perspective. It evaluates the present conditions of the law and practices in this respect. In order to give complete shape to the thesis, a range of research methods are used:

- Review of secondary literature and international instruments on human rights of the accused;
- Examination of the constitutional guarantees regarding the rights of the accused in Bangladesh;
- Analysis of statutory law and case law relating to criminal justice administration in Bangladesh and some other major legal systems, e.g., UK, USA, India and Pakistan;
- Review of relevant public records, available statistical data and annual reports of various human rights organisations;
- Case studies of specific incidents relating to the human rights of the accused; and collection and analysis of relevant data.

Discussion on the conceptual issues in sections 1.2, 1.3 and 1.4 based on the secondary literature including books, journals, electronic materials, constitutional law, statutory law and case law of different countries e.g., UK, USA, India and Pakistan. In one instance Law of Japan has been cited in chapter 3 and in another instance Law of Russia has been cited in chapter 4 for exigency. In addition, references have been made to the 'case law' of the UN Human Rights Committee[19] both in connection with the reporting procedure under Article 40 of the ICCPR and in connection with the consideration of individual communications by the HRC under the Optional Protocol 1.

Study Design: The study is empirical, comparative and at the same time it focuses on previous records and future possibilities.

Period of Study: The study covers a 10 (ten) years period from 1990 to 2000. This period is chosen because from its independence to 1990 Bangladesh experienced military rule for a mentionable period. After the abolition of dictatorial government, 1991 was the starting point of parliamentarian form of government in the real sense. This study concentrates on the above-mentioned period to highlight actual position of human rights of the accused under its prevailing Constitution, laws and practices thereof under the two regimes namely, Khaleda Zia regime (1991-1995) and Shiekh Hasina regime (1996-2000). As the study is completed in the year 2005, important incidents and case laws of the following years, i.e., from 2001 to 2005, have been referred as and where it is felt necessary.

SOURCES AND MODES OF DATA COLLECTION

The study is based on both primary and secondary data. The primary data is collected from field survey. An interview schedule was used as a technique of primary data collection. The researcher visited the courts and police administration for collecting information through formal personal interview with responsible persons. The secondary data is collected from the literature on the topic, Annual Reports of major non-governmental organizations i.e., "Bangladesh Manobadhikar Shamannoy Parishad (BMSP)", Bangladesh Rehabilitation Centre for Trauma Victims (BRCT), Bangladesh Legal Aid and Services Trust (BLAST), Ain O' Shalish Kendra (ASK), Odhikar etc. as well as international organizations and documents i.e., Amnesty International, Human Rights Watch, UDHR, ICCPR etc. Moreover, information have been collected from the website of various national and international organizations. The researcher himself has studied some important cases on groups and individual participants. The collected data are classified, analysed and tabulated according to the different objectives and variables of the study.

On the basis of the evaluation some proposals by way of recommendations have been made in the conclusion of each chapter to improve the conditions of criminal justice system administration in Bangladesh. An overall conclusion has been drawn in chapter seven as a summary of the recommendations made in each chapter.

In respect of citation in this study, it is to be noted that all references from books, article of journals or other sources collected from hard copy or from electronic resources are cited in the footnotes in the following order, surname, initial given name(s), publishers, year of publication and page number or paragraph number. In referencing electronic materials in most cases the paragraph number is cited. The Uniform Resource Locator (URL) of each electronic source is followed by the address.

SCOPES AND LIMITATION OF THE STUDY

It was seen in sections 1.2, 1.3, and 1.4 that the concepts of the rights of the accused encompass a wide range of elements out of which the scope of this study is related to two things namely, right of the accused at the pre-trial and trial stages both in international and Bangladesh perspective. While discussing international aspect basically the UDHR and ICCPR have been emphasised. In making comparison between the international and domestic perspective instances of some countries like UK, USA, India and Pakistan have relatively been focussed.

The scope of the study relates to the administration of justice in Bangladesh and ranges for a period of ten years i.e., from 1990 to 2000. This study is not the result of a Government assignment, but it is a spontaneous research work for which the proposal made in different chapters are of recommendatory nature and it is intended to pave the way for the Government to take necessary steps in protecting the rights of the accused.

RATIONALES AND JUSTIFICATION OF THE STUDY

It is hoped that this study will make a significant contribution to the concepts of the human rights of the accused. It will help the policy makers, legislators and researchers to know about the problems and prospects of the rights of the accused. The findings of this study are intended to help the government to improve the existing laws relating to the criminal justice in Bangladesh.

As the study is concerned with the violation of the rights of the accused and protections thereof, as well as the effectiveness of laws, steps of Government, awareness of people and respect to laws, which are the glaring issues of day, it deserves some inordinate significance. It is a new combination for the researcher, because as far as known, there has been no research work done as yet on this matter in Bangladesh.

It is expected that this recent issue can be treated as an important and valuable source for the workers on this subject. Undoubtedly protection of the rights of the accused has been a burning issue in Bangladesh. Results of this research are of much value in giving some light to the promotion and protection of the rights of the accused against any kind of unscrupulous activities of the LEA. The findings of the research will be helpful for the people, especially the accused who may be inflicted in a case or detained in custody; further an accused will get encouraged to find ways for establishing his/her rights.

Moreover, it will open wide opportunities for other researchers concerned with this arena. This research work may be helpful for the students of law to enrich their knowledge. Besides, many institutions, agencies and organizations will benefit from this type of new research work.

REVIEW OF LITERATURE

Since criminal justice administration is a fast growing subject and wherein interaction of the three Governments organs i.e., executive, legislature and judiciary in a democratic state has become a subject of discussion and research from the days of the formation of the democratic government in society innumerable books and articles are written on this topic. But because of the changing patterns of the society and human behaviour with the development of science and technology earlier literature on this topic is becoming insufficient to give exact information and protection. Moreover, most of the previous literature is written by persons who have legal teaching background without any practical knowledge. Thus, many books regarding criminal justice administration are found in different libraries; and mostly some aspects of the activities of the LEA are found in *Police Regulations of Bengal, Criminal Justice System Administration* and *Police Administration in Bangladesh.* But none of them contains any adequate information about what Bangladeshi readers need to know on the topic of human rights of the accused.

On the legal relationship some other books, which bears much significance, are being stated below in brief.

Protection of Human Rights in Criminal Justice Administration

Manjula Batra in the book named *Protection of Human Rights in Criminal Justice Administration* has made a comparative study of the Indian criminal justice system, which is based on common law system with the Soviet criminal justice system, which is based on socialist law. She has discussed the procedural guarantees accorded to the accused under Indian and Soviet legal systems. The author has focused on the pre-trial stage rights of the accused i.e., right to freedom from unwanted arrest; right to reasonable investigation; interrogation; search and seizure; right to legal defence and fair pre-trial detention and finally right to public and speedy trial.

Criminal Justice System Administration

Dr. M. Enamul Huq in the book *Criminal Justice System Administration* has made a combined discussion on Police, Prosecution, Court and Correctional system. He has emphasized upon international police co-operation to prevent multinational terrorism or crime; drug offences and transborder human trafficking. The author has focused light on prison condition, common peoples participation in preventing crime, public awareness against corruption, role of police in protecting human rights and role of Bangladesh Police in international area.

Police Administration in Bangladesh

ABMG Kibria in the book named *Police Administration in Bangladesh* has dealt with the historical origin of policing in Indian-sub-continent. He has discussed about the composition of police administration, training methodology, personal management, police communication and investigation procedure. The author has mentioned the role of police in traffic control, patrol, strikes, riots, crowd control and disaster planning. He has also sketched a relationship between police and public.

Criminal Investigation

The book *Criminal Investigation* by John Adam and John Collyer Adam is a practical textbook for all who are charged with the duty of investigating crime under a charged social order particularly after the infusion of science in the field of crime. The book focuses on inevitability of specialist as clue finder for the sake of justice. This book is destined to show the manner of handling various forms of crime and explaining motives. This book has been designed as a working handbook for all engaged in the criminal investigation by suggesting them about how source could assist in investigation without interrupting some rights of the citizen. It also provides advice in respect of examination of witnesses and accused and the inspection of localities.

Constitutional Law of Bangladesh

In the book *Constitutional Law of Bangladesh,* Mahmudul Islam has discussed constitution, constitutional laws and some other aspects related to the criminal justice administration. This book may provide a good knowledge about the constitutional laws of Bangladesh but will hardly fulfil the academic thirst of readers concerning the subject matter of the study.

Apart from these works, a list of other books, articles, documents, statutes, and journals on different aspects of the rights of the accused may be found but none of them has dealt with this research topic in the light and details as it has been done in this work. In none of them could be found an unbiased and in-depth treatment of this burning research area. Attempts have been made in this work to suggest reform where necessary and update the existing laws so that an effective and efficient criminal justice system is ensured in a fitful way.

ORGANISATION OF THE STUDY

The study has been devoted mainly towards assessing the implementation of international human rights instruments regarding rights of the accused and role of the Governments, especially LEA in controlling crime and preserve human rights of the accused in Bangladesh. To highlight the issues the whole research work has been divided into SEVEN chapters and each of the chapters contains the details of the subject discussed thereunder.

The first chapter is introductory with description of the crime situation prevailing in Bangladesh. This chapter outlines the aims and methods of the study. It discusses the scope and limits of the study, the objectives of the study, the research methodology and the review of literature.

The second chapter provides with the constitutional guarantees of the accused. This chapter identifies the links between human rights and the constitutional guarantees. In this chapter, endeavours have been made to disclose how far the basic human rights of an accused as guaranteed in Bangladesh are implemented and how far the accused are enjoying their rights as free citizens.

The third chapter focuses on the rights of arrested and detained persons with special reference to the state of preventive detention under the SPA and the role of police in Bangladesh. It highlights the role of police as the main LEA in the protection of human rights in Bangladesh.

The fourth chapter deals with the rights that accrue to the accused while he/she is being subjected to investigation, questioning, search and seizure. In this chapter a discussion has been made on criminal legislation, right to protection from, and evidentiary value of, unlawful search and seizure.

The fifth chapter deals with the right to a fair trial and rights of prisoners in Bangladesh. This chapter highlights the rights available to the accused at the under-trial stage and also discusses the prisoners' rights including the jail situation in Bangladesh.

The sixth chapter attempts to elucidate the meaning of arrest and shows the state of human rights in Bangladesh. This chapter is based on interviews with the accused, lawyers, judicial officers and police officers.

The seventh and last chapter presents a general conclusion including the findings and recommendations in the light of findings. The recommendations are made to update the existing laws to provide due and just relief to those who are aggrieved by the arbitrary exercise of powers of the LEA.

Every chapter specially deals with issues relating to the rights of the women accused. It clarifies what types of rights the women accused are entitled to. The objective of this section is to ponder over those rights guaranteed to a woman accused in criminal justice.

CONCLUSION

This study presents an evaluation of the existing conditions of the criminal justice administration in Bangladesh. As discussed in sections1.8 and 1.9 the study concentrates on the human rights of the accused in pre-trial and trial stages.

The final chapter summarises the major findings of the study and outlines the possible recommendations to strengthen the criminal justice in order to establish human rights of the accused.

NOTES

1. M. Ershadul Bari, 'The Universal Declaration of Human Rights— *The Magna Carta* of Mankind' in *Human Rights in Contemporary International Law,* (Dhaka: 1995), 27.
2. *Human Rights Today*-UN Briefing Papers, (UN Publications: October, 1998), 6.
3. Manjula Batra, *Protection of Human Rights in Criminal Justice Administration,* (Deep & Deep Publications, New Delhi: 1989), 7.
4. *Hereinafter referred to as* the UDHR.
5. *Hereinafter referred to as* the ICCPR or the Covenant. The Covenant is the component of the International Bill of Human Rights, which

were adopted unanimously by 106 States on December 1966 and entered into force in 1976. In 2000 Bangladesh acceded to the ICCPR considered by the human rights experts as the most influential human rights mechanism of the United Nations. Through this ratification Bangladesh has undertaken to respect and to ensure all individuals within its territory and subject to its jurisdiction the rights recognized in the Covenant without discrimination of any kind.

6. See *supra note* 2 at 6.
7. Hobbs T., *Leviathan,* (Aldinepress, Letchworth: 1914), 63.
8. Salmond WG, *Jurisprudence,* (12th Edition; Maxwell: 1985), 89.
9. Third degree method means a method in which the police apply physical and/or mental pressure upon the suspect to exact information of incriminatory nature while he/she is being interrogated. *See also* Chapter 4.3.
10. *Hereinafter referred to as* the Cr. P. C. *or* the Code.
11. Batra, M, *supra note* 3 at 3.
12. *International Covenant on Civil and Political Rights (ICCPR)* 1966, Article 14(2).
13. *Universal Declaration of Human Rights (UDHR)* 1948, Article 3.
14. *International Covenant on Civil and Political Rights (ICCPR)* 1966, Article 6.
15. *Anwar Hossain Chowdhury vs. Bangladesh,* 41 DLR (AD) 165.
16. Mahmudul Islam, *Constitutional Law of Bangladesh,* (BILIA Publication, Dhaka: 1995), 16.
17. *Hereinafter referred to as* the SPA.
18. M. Faiz-ud-Din and MA Hannan, 'Protection of Human Rights in Criminal Justice: Bangladesh Perspective', *Research Project,* 1998, (Rajshahi University, Bangladesh), 2; *see also* Chapter 3.9.
19. *Hereinafter referred to as* the HRC *or* the Committee.

CONSTITUTIONAL GUARANTEES OF THE ACCUSED 2

INTRODUCTION

In 1971 Bangladesh emerged as an independent state through a long struggle of 9 months' war and it received recognition by different states.[1] The noble purpose behind this war was to establish a just and democratic society in which all citizens will enjoy fundamental rights without any discrimination. With this end in view, Bangladesh framed a Constitution in which civil, political, economic, social and cultural rights were guaranteed so that people could live with peace and harmony.

The Constitution is not only the principal document of a state to regulate the state machinery but also the supreme law of the land which guarantees the fundamental human rights without which a man cannot live like a human being. Human rights and fundamental freedoms help us to develop our human qualities, consciousness and personality, which are essential to satisfy our physical and spiritual needs. The presence of a Constitution therefore, is a must and without Constitution the concepts of a modern democratic state cannot be imagined.

Before understanding fundamental rights one should have idea about human rights. The term 'human rights' does not mean any right used in a special sense. Human rights are those legal and moral rights, which can be claimed by any person for the very reason that he is a human being. These rights come with birth and are applicable to all people throughout the world irrespective of their race, colour, sex, language or political or other opinion. These are, therefore, those rights that are inherent in human person and without which they cannot live as human being.

The term fundamental right is a technical one, for when certain human rights are written down in a constitution and are protected by constitutional guarantees, they are called fundamental rights in the sense that they are placed in the supreme or fundamental law of the land which has a supreme sanctity over all other laws of the land.

After the adoption of UDHR in 1948, most of the democratic states of the world inserted in their Constitutions some rights in the name of fundamental rights or fundamental human rights. These rights are basic rights without which a citizen cannot enjoy the life of a free citizen as because these rights are essential for human beings. Taking into consideration the provisions of the UDHR, Bangladesh framed a Constitution, which came into force on 16 December 1972.

The important fundamental rights, which every citizen is entitled, are enshrined in part III of the Constitution of Bangladesh. The provisions of this part shall prevail upon other laws, which are inconsistent with these provisions. In this respect Article 26(1) of the Constitution of Bangladesh states, "All existing law inconsistent with the provisions of this part shall, to the extent of such inconsistency become void on the commencement of this Constitution". So it is clear that the provisions embodied in part III will prevail over any other existing laws of the land.

In this chapter, endeavours have been made to disclose how far the basic human rights of an accused as guaranteed by the Constitution and different statutes in Bangladesh are implemented and whether the accused is enjoying his/her rights like a free citizen or is being deprived of some of the fundamental rights either in part or in full. Attention has been drawn to see the real picture of the accused who become the victim of deprivation due to miscarriage of justice or due to misuse of power by the LEA. Examination on some provisions of part III of the Constitution will be made in order to find out the actual state of human rights in Bangladesh, which will help to ameliorate the deteriorating condition of human rights of the accused.

EQUALITY BEFORE LAW

The Constitution of Bangladesh states, "All citizens are equal before law and are entitled to equal protection of law".[2] It is one of the important fundamental rights that a citizen must enjoy. Fair and impartial application of these fundamental rights is some times found to be absent at the time of disposal of cases especially at the time of granting bail to the accused. An accused is sometimes granted bail by applying undue influence whereas another accused is not granted bail in the same nature of case. A glaring example of exercising such influence may be cited to bear the testimony of the fact. A Member of Parliament (MP), Alamgir Kabir of Nowgaon District was arrested on 10 April 1999 on suspicion that he was involved in a murder case of two political leaders of the same district. He was not granted bail by the lower court and as such he could not join the session of the Parliament.[3] On the contrary an MP of Moulovi Bazar, Mujibur Rahman (Manik), was arrested in 1999 for an incident, which took place in his residence where some bombs explored at the time of their preparation, and two persons involved in the incident were killed. Killing of two persons and explosion of bombs are two separate penal offences, which took place in the residence of the said MP. He was arrested on the above charge; but shortly thereafter he was granted bail by the lower court and so he got the opportunity to join the session of the Parliament. This shows the discriminating behaviour of the courts and thus the provision of Article 27 of the Constitution has been violated. Of course, Alamgir Kabir was granted bail by the High Court Division (HCD) on 9 August 1999 and he was released from the Dhaka Central Jail on 27 August 1999.[4] So in a similar case, one has been granted bail by the lower court, but the other accused has been granted bail by the HCD and as a result one was detained in the jail for a longer period than the other. Is it not discriminatory and a clear violation of the Constitutional provision? This is one of the many examples of the violation of Article 27.

In another incident in Jessore district some accused against whom warrant was issued were set free from Jessore Sub-jail without observing legal formalities, though regular case was lodged against them.[5] According to a report of the police authority, 248 persons were arrested under Section 54 of the Cr. P. C. 221 persons were granted bail on 13 July 1999. But some other persons were set free including two top terrors against whom there were different charges including murder. This is against the principle of equality before law. Criminals, whoever they may be, whatever influential persons they may be, must follow the definite principle so that the accused may not be the victims of discrimination. In the above cases, it has been found that the constitutional provision of equal protection of law has been defeated.

PROTECTION OF LAW

Article 31 of the Constitution of Bangladesh provides that "To enjoy the protection of the law and to be treated in accordance with law, and only in accordance with law, is the inalienable right of every citizen, wherever he may be, and of every other person for the time being within Bangladesh and in particular no action detrimental to the life, liberty, body, reputation or property of any other person shall be taken except in accordance with law". This Article declares two fundamental rights; first, to enjoy the protection of law, and to be treated in accordance with law, is the inalienable right of every citizen. Second, no action detrimental to the life, liberty, body, reputation or property of any person shall be taken except in accordance with law.

These provisions are co-related with the subsequent Article in which it is declared, "No person shall be deprived of life or personal liberty save in accordance with law".[6] Right to life is an inherent right of a man. Because no man can take away the life of other man capriciously this right has been guaranteed with a great accentuation by all national, regional and international law, custom, usage etc. Article 3 of the UDHR states that "Everyone has the right to life". The ICCPR has stated vividly the right to life.[7]

Every accused being a human being has the inherent right to life. This right shall be protected by law. No one shall be arbitrarily deprived of his/her life. The death penalty can only be carried out pursuant to a final judgement rendered by a competent court. The European Convention on Human Rights and Fundamental Freedoms (ECHR) also speaks against arbitrary deprivation of life.[8] It states that "Every one's right to life shall be protected by law. No one shall be deprived of his life intentionally save in the execution of a sentence of a court following his conviction of a crime for which this penalty is provided by law".[9] The American Declaration of the Rights and Duties of Man and the American Convention on Human Rights, 1969 (ACHR) also advocated against arbitrary deprivation of life saying that, "Every human being has the right to life".[10]

Every person has the right to have his life respected. This right shall be protected by law, and in general, from the moment of conception. No one shall be deprived of his life. Every person condemned to death shall have the right to apply for amnesty, pardon or commutation of sentence, which may be granted in all cases. Capital punishment shall not be imposed while such a petition is pending by the competent authority".[11] The African Charter on Human and Peoples' Right also upholds the right to life. It says, "Human rights are inviolable. Every human being shall be entitled to respect for his life and the integrity of his personality. No one may be arbitrarily deprived of right".[12]

Regarding the protection of life and personal liberty Constitution of India states that, "No person shall be deprived of his life or personal liberty except according to procedure established by law".[13] In the like manner, Constitution of Pakistan provides that "No person shall be deprived of life or liberty save in accordance with law".[14]

Despite the protections mentioned above in the Constitution of Bangladesh the right to life of an accused is being violated by the LEA like Police, BDR, ANSAR and RAB.

It has been reported by the national dailies and the non-governmental organisations that rampant human rights violations are taking place across the country. In 1996, 43 persons were killed by firing of the LEA.[15] in 1997, 57 persons were killed under the custody of LEA, 23 died in jail custody, 28 by police firing and 6 died by police torture and 163 received bullet injury by police, BDR and ANSAR.[16] In 1998, 56 prisoners died under police and jail custody,[17] among them 14 under police custody, 1 under BDR custody and 41 died more or less by torture by jail and police authority. Another Report of BRCT[18] discloses the fact that from January 1998 to June 1998, fifteen persons were killed by torture by the LEA, 28 killed by firing, 4 persons died under police custody, 25 persons in jail custody, 17 raped by police, 55 injured seriously by law enforcing agencies and the number of tortured persons by them is 152. In 2002 number of custodial deaths is 38.[19] This is absolutely shocking for the nation. Even the President of the country in a speech delivered in 8th National Conference on Human Rights, had to say that torture and inhuman treatment meted out to a person in custody and custodial death are against humanity and civilization.[20] In the year 2004 the LEA especially RAB killed people in the name of crossfire that caused death of some 70 people across the country since June to December.[21] This information bear the testimony that the right to life, liberty, body, reputation or property of an accused is being violated in spite of ensuring these rights under Articles 31 and 32 of the Constitution of Bangladesh.

Grounds of Arrest or Detention and Consultation with Lawyer

Article 33(1) and (2) of the Constitution of Bangladesh make provisions against arbitrary arrest and detention saying that, "No person who is arrested shall be detained in custody without being informed, as soon as may be, of the grounds for such arrest, nor shall he be denied the right to consult and be defended by a legal practitioner of his choice".[22] Again this Article says, "Every person who is arrested and detained in custody shall be produced before the nearest Magistrate within a period of twenty four hours of such arrest excluding the time necessary for the journey from the place of arrest to the court of the magistrate, and no such person shall be detained in custody beyond the said period without the authority of a magistrate".[23] This Article is in the line of the UDHR, which states, "No one shall be subjected to arbitrary arrest, detention or exile."[24]

These fundamental rights of an accused are being violated by the LEA in Bangladesh. By taking advantages of some other provisions of Cr. P. C. the police infringe the fundamental rights of the accused. One of the most controversial provisions is Section 54 of Cr. P. C. For proper appreciation, Section 54 of the Code is reproduced below:

> "Any Police Officer, may, without an order from a Magistrate and without warrant, arrest-*first of all,* any person who has been concerned in any cognisable offence or against whom a reasonable complaint has been made or credible information has been received or a reasonable suspicion exists of his having been concerned; *secondly,* any person having in his possession without lawful excuse, the burden of proving which excuse shall lie on such person, any implementation of house breaking; *thirdly,* any person who has been proclaimed as an offender either under this Code or by order of the government; *fourthly,* any person in whose possession anything is found which may reasonably be suspected to be stolen property and who may reasonably be suspected of having committed an offence with reference to such thing; *fifthly,* any person who obstructs a Police Officer while in the execution of his duty, or who has escaped, or attempts to escape, from lawful custody; *sixthly,* any person reasonably suspected or being a deserter from the Armed Forces of Bangladesh; *seventhly,* any person who has been concerned in or against whom a reasonable complaint has been made or credible information has been received or a reasonable suspicion exists of his having been concerned in any act committed at any place out of Bangladesh, which, if committed in Bangladesh, would have been punishable as an offence,

and for which he is, under any law relating to extradition under the Fugitive Offenders Act, 1881 or otherwise liable to be apprehended or detained in custody in Bangladesh; *eighthly,* any released convict committing a breach of any rule made under Section 565(3); *ninthly,* any person for whose arrest a requisition has been received from another Police Officer, provided that the requisition specified the person to be arrested and the offence or other cause for which the arrest is to be made and it appears therefrom that the person might lawfully be arrested without a warrant by an officer who issued the requisition."

On the above nine clauses the Police Officer may arrest any person without warrant. But from clause one it is possible to articulate four conditions, which are couched in such words that there is scope of an abusive and colourable exercise of power. Following are the four conditions, which are included in the first clause. The Police Officer may arrest (a) any person who has been concerned in any cognisable offence; (b) against whom a reasonable complaint has been made; (c) a credible information has been received; and (d) against whom a reasonable suspicion exists of his having been so concerned in any cognisable offence.

The word 'concerned' used in first clause is a vague word which gives unhindered power to a police officer to arrest any person stating that the person arrested by him is 'concerned' in a cognisable offence. From the language of Section 54 of the Cr. P. C. it is found that, the Police Officer can exercise the power in abuse. There is nothing in this Section, which provides that the accused should be furnished with the grounds for his arrest, although it is the basic human right that whenever a person is arrested he must know the reasons for his arrest. Under Section 54, a Police Officer does not disclose the reasons for the arrest to the person whom he/she has arrested, but earlier mentioned clause (1) of Article 33 of the Constitution mentioned earlier provides that the person who is arrested shall be informed of the grounds for such arrest. It is true that no time limit has been mentioned in this Article but the expression "as soon as may be" is used which does not mean that furnishing of grounds may be delayed for an indefinite period. Justice Md. Hamidul Haque in *BLAST*[25] case states that "As soon as may be" implies that the grounds shall be furnished after the person is brought to the police station after his arrest and entries are made in the diary about his arrest. Unfortunately, this provision of the Constitution is not followed by the police officers. It is strange that they are very much over zealous in exercising the powers given under Section 54 but they are reluctant to act in accordance with the provisions of the Constitution itself. It is strange that instead of adhering to the provisions of the Constitution the Police Officers are interested in exercising the powers given to them under the Code without any hesitation. And more strangely our government is ratifying such practice. It is evident to anyone if he/she observes the mass arrest made under Section 54 during the tenure of each government in various times to suppress the political opponents.

The Constitution not only provides that the person arrested shall be informed of the grounds for his/her arrest, it also provides that the person arrested shall not be denied the right to consult and to defend him/herself by a legal practitioner of his choice. In *BLAST case* it was opined that immediately after furnishing the grounds for arrest to the person, the police should be bound to provide the facility to the person to consult his lawyer if he desires so. But the persons arrested by the police under Section 54 are not being allowed to enjoy this constitutional right. Not only this right is denied, even the police refuses to inform the nearest or close relatives of the person arrested. Justice Hamidul Haque in this case is of the view that the person arrested shall be allowed to enjoy these rights immediately after he is brought to the police station from the place of arrest and before he is produced to the nearest Magistrate so that he can defend himself properly.

The right of representation by a lawyer is often considered to be a part of natural justice. If the person is denied the service of a spokesman, it will be a clear violation of natural justice. In *Pett vs. Greyhound Racing Assn (1)*,[26] Lord Denning observed:

> "When a Man's reputation or livelihood is at stake, he not only has a right to speak by his own mouth. He has also a right to speak by counsel or solicitor ....". Even a prisoner can have his friend."

Recently a case[27] was sent back for fresh trial by the HCD on the ground of denial of representation. The prosecution case, in brief, was that on 20 September 1984 at night accused Babu Khan entered the house of one Alauddin Khan. He along with his wife caught hold of accused Babu Khan and then Babu Khan assaulted them indiscriminately with dagger and fled away. Jarina Khatun wife of Alauddin Khan could recognise Babu Khan in the light of *kupibati*. The victims Alauddin Khan and his wife were taken to hospital for treatment. On 22 September 1984 Alauddin Khan succumbed to the injuries and out of the occurrence one Abdur Rajjaque neighbour of the victims, lodged the First Information Report (FIR) on 21 September 1984. After investigation the police submitted charge sheet against the accused Babu Khan on 2 November 1984 under Section 380/511/459/326/302 of the Penal Code and that the case thereafter was sent to the Court of Session for trial. The learned Sessions Judge on 7 January 1986 framed charge against the accused under Sections 302/326 of the Penal Code in absence of the accused and made an order convicting him.

The accused filed an appeal to the HCD against his conviction order under Section 302 of the Penal Code. The HCD opined that the accused admittedly being in abscondence ought to have been defended by the lawyer at the cost of the State under chapter XII of the Legal Remembrance Manual (LRM). As there was no such appointment of any lawyer the trial from the beginning has been absolutely illegal and hence the impugned judgment and order cannot sustain in the eye of law.

The Legal Remembrance Manual provides that, "every person charged with committing an offence punishable with death, shall have legal assistance at his trial and the court should provide advocate or pleader for the defence unless they certify that the accused can afford to do so.[28] It is thus provided that every person charged with committing any offence punishable with death shall be given legal assistance at his trial. In this connection the judges of the above-discussed case quote Section 340 of the Cr. P. C., which runs as follows:

> "Any person accused of an offence before a criminal court or against whom proceedings are instituted under this Code in any such court, may as of right be defended by an advocate."[29]

Thus under Section 340 of the Cr. P. C. and Article 33 of the Constitution of Bangladesh the right to consult and to be defended by a legal practitioner has been guaranteed. So the right of an accused to be defended by a lawyer in a case charged under Section 302 of the Penal Code being punishable with death, is an inalienable right guaranteed in the law of our land and if any trial takes place in refusing such fundamental right the trial is a misnomer and the judgement passed in such trial convicting an accused is no judgement in the eye of law.

In this connection the decision in the case of *The State vs. Imdad Ali Bepary*[30] may be referred to wherein their lordships held:

> "In this case it appears that no lawyer on behalf of the accused was present in court. As such, the lower court, before proceeding with the case ought to have appointed an advocate to defend the accused. In that view of the said illegality the conviction and sentence of the condemned prisoner under Section 302 is not maintainable and therefore set aside and the case is sent back for re-trial to the lower court, for appointing an Advocate to represent the accused and given him a chance to cross-examine the witnesses adduced in the case."

In another decision in case of *Mobarak Ali (Md) alias Mobarak Ali Mondal vs. People's Republic of Bangladesh,* represented by the Ministry of Home Affairs Secretary it has been observed,

> "We hold that the requirements of law is that irrespective of whether the accused is absconding or

> not he is as of right entitled to be represented by the court and the trial court must ensure that it has been done before the commencement of the trial or else the trial and the resultant conviction and sentence would be initiated."[31]

The right to consult with the lawyer is also approved by some Indian case decisions. The right of the accused to consult his legal advisor and to be defended by him has been put at the highest footing under Article 33 of the Constitution of India and it is really not necessary to deduce it new from other enactments.[32] Section 340 of the Code has been expressly made applicable not only to person accused of an offence but also to any person against whom proceedings are instituted under the Code in any criminal court.[33] The government is entitled as of right to be heard by counsel or advocate in support of the prosecution whether in original or in appellate court. The accused is entitled to be represented by an advocate. This is a privilege given to him. The only duty cast on the court is to afford him the necessary opportunity.[34] When a person is not defended, the judge should make arrangement for his defence in grave cases. In cases where a lawyer has been engaged to defend the prisoner at the expense of the government, the trial judge must see that a greater experienced advocate is appointed to cross examine the witness. Section 340 of the Cr. P. C. implies that the accused shall have a reasonable opportunity, if in custody, to communicate with his advocate and prepare for his defence.[35] Full opportunity should be afforded to the accused to get proper legal advice and assistance before he is called upon to cross-examine the prosecution witnesses.[36]

There are sufficient case decisions on this point in Bangladesh. In *Sate vs. Abdul Gazi,*[37] it was held that Section 340 of the Cr. P. C. confers a right on every accused person brought before a criminal court to be defended by a lawyer. The accused must be afforded full opportunity to be properly defended and he has a right to be defended by a lawyer of his choice. The denial of this right must be held to have rendered the trial as one not according to law and necessitated a fresh trial. Failure to comply with the prayer of the accused to recall prosecution witnesses for cross examination on material points by the newly engaged lawyer after the withdrawal of the previous defence lawyer prejudice the accused.

In *Abdul Gani vs. The State*[38] the judges enunciated that accused has a right to be defended at the State's cost. Brief must be supplied and proper opportunity be given for the lawyer to make himself ready. It is the responsibility of the court to engage a lawyer for an undefended accused.

In *Abdul Mannan vs. The State,*[39] it was said that an accused has got the legal right of advancing arguments before the trying Magistrate. The right of being defended by an advocate means the right of making such representations or submission to the court as may be available to an accused person for meeting the charges levelled against him.

In *The State vs. Rabiul Hossain alias Rob*[40] the condemned prisoner was in custody. He was produced before the court from time to time; but he was not represented by any lawyer of his choice. The court observed that it was the duty of the court to appoint a lawyer at the cost of the State to defend the condemned prisoner, as the offence was punishable with death. It will allow the accused to be aware of the grounds for his arrest and get the help of a lawyer by consulting him. If these two rights are denied, this will amount to confining him in custody beyond the authority of the Constitution.

Article 33 clause II of the Constitution of Bangladesh articulates the time limit within which an accused is to be produced to the nearest Magistrate. When a person who is arrested under Section 54 without a warrant, the provisions of Section 61 of the Cr. P. C. applies in this case. It provides that no Police Officer shall detain in custody a person arrested without warrant for a period exceeding 24 hours unless there is a special order of a Magistrate under Section 167 of the Code.[41] So there is a reference of Section 167, in Section 61 of the Code, which provides, if there is a special order of a Magistrate under Section 167, the police may keep a person in its custody for more than 24 hours. In *Abdur Rahman vs. The*

State[42] it was held that production of the accused before Magistrate does not amount to taking cognisance of any offence by him/her. Under Section 61 it is provided that no Police Officer shall detain in custody a person arrested without warrant for a longer period than under all the circumstances of the case is reasonable and such period shall not, in the absence of a special order of a Magistrate under Section 167, exceed twenty-four hours excluding of the time necessary for the journey from the place of arrest to the Magistrate.

Upholding the Constitutional provision in *Mehnaz Sakib vs. Bangladesh*[43] case, it was stated that since the detainee was arrested under Section 54 of the Cr. P. C. it was incumbent upon the police to produce her before a Magistrate within twenty-four hours but the police having not done so, the right guaranteed to her under the Constitution has been violated.

It is necessary to peruse what is provided in Section 167 of the Cr. P. C. Relevant provisions of this Section are produced below:

"Procedure when investigation cannot be completed in twenty-four hours–

whenever any person is arrested and detained in custody, and it appears that the investigation cannot be completed within the period of twenty-four hours fixed by Section 61, and there are grounds for believing that the accusation or information is well-founded, the Officer-in-charge of the police station of the police Officer making the investigation if he is not below the rank of Sub-inspector shall forthwith transmit to the nearest Magistrate a copy of the entries in the diary hereinafter prescribed relating to the case, and shall at the same time forward the accused to such Magistrate.

The Magistrate to whom an accused person is forwarded under this section may, whether he has or has not jurisdiction to try the case, from time to time, authorise the detention of the accused in such custody as such Magistrate thinks fit, for a term not exceeding fifteen days in the whole. If he has not jurisdiction to try the case or send it for trial, and considers further detention unnecessary, he may order the accused to be forwarded to a Magistrate having such jurisdiction.

Provided that no Magistrate of the third class, and no Magistrate of the second class not specially empowered in this behalf by the Government shall authorise detention in the custody of the police.

A Magistrate authorising under this Section detention in the custody of the police shall record his reasons for so doing.

If such order is given by a Magistrate other than the Chief Metropolitan Magistrate (CMM), District Magistrate (DM) or Sub-divisional Magistrate, he shall forward a copy of his order, with his reasons for making it, to the Magistrate to whom he is immediately sub-ordinate".

From the above provision it stands that if the requirements of sub-section (1) are not fulfilled, the Magistrate cannot pass an order under Sub-section (2) for detaining a person exceeding twenty-four hours. But such practice is being exercised under the title of remand.[44]

Before entering into the aspect of custodial death it is necessary to give a definition of police custody. Police custody means and includes, custody under the authority of the police—every person who is kept in attendance to answer a charge in such a way that he is practically deprived of his freedom.[45] In such custody during the past few years, the numbers of deaths have attracted the attention of the press, human rights groups and international agencies. During the *Operation Clean Heart* in 2002 as many as 47 people were reportedly killed in police custody.[46] In the year 2003, 115 persons were killed in 95 occurrences in several places of Bangladesh by law enforcement and security personnel. Out of these numbers 27 people were killed in custody.[47]

PREVENTIVE DETENTION

In original Constitution of Bangladesh, Article 33 did not leave any scope for preventive detention. But by second amendment of the Constitution, Article 33 was replaced by the present one. It provides that safeguard of Articles 33(1) (2) will not be available in the case of arrested persons under any law of preventive detention. But the Constitution has imposed some restrictions upon exercising such law. In order to protect the individuals from arbitrary arrest and detention by the executive Articles 33(4), 33(5) provide 3 important safeguards.

Approval by Advisory Board

No law providing for preventive detention shall authorise the detention of a person for a period exceeding six months unless an Advisory Board[48] consisting of three persons, of whom two shall be persons who are, or have been, or are qualified to be appointed as, Judges of the Supreme Court and the other shall be a person who is a Senior Officer in the service of the Republic, has, after affording him an opportunity of being heard in person, reported before the expiration of the said period of six months that there is in its opinion, sufficient cause for such detention.[49]

Right to Communication of Grounds of Detention

When any person is detained in pursuance of an order made under any law providing for preventive detention, the authority making the order shall, as soon as may be, communicate to such person the grounds on which the order has been made.[50]

Right to Representation Against Order of Detention

The authority making the order of detention shall afford the detainee the earliest opportunity of making a representation against the order. The right to representation against order of detention depends on the right to communication of grounds of detention. Because in order to make an effective representation detainee must know the grounds. But proviso to Article 33(5) and proviso of Section 8 (1) of the SPA state, the authority making any such order may refuse to disclose facts, which such authority considers to be against the public interest to disclose. Here lies the crux of the problem. The authority takes this opportunity and often decline to communicate the grounds to the detainee. So, the constitutional safeguards have become meaningless. Again the AB is not a judicial body; though it is constituted under the provision of the Constitution of Bangladesh, it follows the executive proceedings rather than judicial proceedings. Because Section 11(4) of the SPA stated that, the detainee against whom a detention order has been made cannot appear by any legal practitioner in any matter connected with the reference to the Advisory Board and the proceedings of the Board and its report, excepting that part of the report in which the opinion of the Board is specified, shall be confidential. As the report of the Board is binding on the executive, it is always influenced by the executive.

Statutory Restrictions

Under the amended provision of Article 33, the Special Powers Act (SPA), 1974 was enacted; there also have some safeguards for the detainee. At first the authority has to prove that the detainee is engaged in any prejudicial act referred in Section 2(f) of the SPA. This Section provides that, "Prejudicial act means any act which is intended or likely:

- to prejudice the sovereignty or defence of Bangladesh;
- to prejudice the maintenance of friendly relation of Bangladesh with foreign states;
- to prejudice the security of Bangladesh or to endanger public safety or the maintenance of public order;
- to create to excite feelings of enmity or hatred between different communities, classes or section of people;
- to interfere with or encourage or incite interference with the administration of law or the maintenance of law and order;
- to prejudice the maintenance of supplies and services essential to the community;
- to cause fear or alarm to the public or to any section of the public;
- to prejudice the economic or financial interests of the State."

A person cannot be detained unless those grounds are satisfied. If the DM or ADM satisfies that the above prejudicial acts exist he can detain any person under Section 3(2) of the

SPA.[51] Section 3(3) of the SPA provides when any order under Sub-section (2) is made, the DM or ADM should forthwith inform the government about the fact of the detention. It should not continue for more than thirty days, if the government does not approve.[52]

In every case where an order has been made under Section 3 of the SPA, the authority making the order shall as soon as may be, communicate to the person affected thereby the grounds on which the order has been made and enable him to make a representation in writing against the order and it shall be the duty of such authority to inform such person of his right of making such representation and to afford him the earliest opportunity of doing so.[53]

In the case of detention order, the authority making the order shall inform the person detained under that order of the grounds of his detention at the time he is detained as soon thereafter as is practicable, but not later than fifteen days from the date of detention.[54]

In every case where a detention order has been made under this Act, the government shall within one hundred and twenty days from the date of the detention order, place before the Advisory Board the ground on which the order has been made and the representation, if any, made by the person affected by the order.[55]

The Advisory Board shall, after considering the materials placed before it and calling for such further information as it may deem necessary from the government or from the person concerned an opportunity of being heard in person, submit its report to the government within one hundred and seventy days from the date of detention.[56] But by expressing the oppressive intention of the executive authority Section 12 of this Act says that in every six months from the date of such detention order the Advisory Board shall, after affording the person concerned an opportunity of being heard in person review such detention order.

By taking the advantages of this SPA, the authority is violating the human rights of the suspects. For a clear conception one of the many examples may be cited here. In

Reita Rahman vs. Bangladesh[57] it was revealed how the executive abuses the provisions of the SPA. In this case, Major Khairuzzaman's detention order by the government was called in question on the ground of non-application of mind. Major Khairuzzaman, the alleged associate in Bangobandhu killing was arrested and detained by the ADM of Dhaka on 13 August 1996 under Section 3(2) of the SPA. The order was signed by the DM on 13 August 1996 and it was served upon the detainee in Dhaka Central Jail on the same day. The grounds of detention were signed by the DM on 26 August 1996 which were served upon the detenu on 27 August 1996. Under Section 3(3) of the SPA the order of detention is to be approved by the government. It appears that the grounds of detention were signed by the DM on 26 August 1996; but the government passed an order of approval and extension of detention on 18 August 1996. So on the face of the record, the grounds of detention were not placed before the government when the government passed the order of extension of detention on 18 August 1996. It was a total absurdity of facts and clear violation of Section 3(3) of the SPA as well as the human rights of the suspect.

In *Zilaluddin vs. Bangladesh*[58] it appears that the order of detention was made on 2 January 2002 but the grounds of detention and the detainee respectively were admittedly placed before the Advisory Board on 15 May 2002 that is on 134th day (counting of days being 2 January 2002 to 15 May 2002, total 134 days) which is after the expiry of one hundred and twenty days as mandated by Section 10 of the SPA. So it was held that the detainee is being detained illegally and improperly on the basis of the recommendation made by the Advisory Board as the grounds of detention and the detainee were not placed before the Advisory Board within 120 days as mandated by Section 10 of the SPA.

Sometimes the ruling party detains their political opponent under Section 3(2) of the SPA by arresting under Section 54 of the Cr. P. C. But it is well known that an arrest under Section 54 of the Cr. P. C. is often a preclude to issuance of detention order under the SPA. The SPA allows the authority to detain any person on eight grounds,[59] vague enough to detain any person, according to the whim and caprice of the executives and the party in power. The use and abuse of the SPA in the name of securing law and order have resulted in steady pattern of human rights violations.

In the case of *Mokbul Hossain vs. Government of Bangladesh and others*[60] Justice Md. Hamidul Haque speaking for the Division Bench observed:

> "We are of the view that after arresting a person under Section 54 of the Cr. P. C. there is no bar that the same person cannot be detained under preventive detention."

However, in a subsequent decision of another Division Bench presided over by the said Judge on the said point in the case of BLAST, different views were expressed which appear to be in conformity with the law than the views expressed in *Mokbul Hossain's* case. In *BLAST* case the Justice opined that a Police Officer might arrest a person under Section 54, under certain conditions. Main condition is that the person arrested is to be concerned in a cognisable offence. So first requirement to arrest a person under Section 54 is that the same person is be engaged in any cognisable offence. The purpose of detention is totally different. A person is detained under the preventive detention law not for his involvement in any offence but for the purpose of preventing him from doing any prejudicial act. So a Police Officer cannot arrest a person under Section 54 of the Cr. P. C. with a view for detaining him/her under Section 3 of the SPA. Such arrest is neither lawful nor permissible under Section 54. If the authority has any reason to detain a person under Section 3 of the SPA, the detention can be made by making an order under the provisions of that Section and when such order is made and handed over to the police for detaining the person, the order shall be treated as warrant of arrest and on the basis of that order, the police may arrest a person for the purpose of detention. It is a proved fact that a person cannot be arrested under Section 54 of the Code for detaining him under Section 3 of the SPA, it is being used though illegally to coerce the suspects.

CRITICISM OF THE PREVENTIVE DETENTION LAW

The preventive detention law is full of negative features:

(i) Both in the Constitution of Pakistan and India the initial period of detention is 3 months. But in the Constitution of Bangladesh the initial period of detention is 6 months. Nowhere in the world such a long period of initial detention is found.

(ii) No maximum period of detention is fixed either in the Constitution or in the SPA. It means that a person can be detained for an indefinite period once the Advisory Board opines that there exists sufficient cause for such detention.

(iii) In democratically developed countries like USA it is specifically mentioned that only in time of emergency, preventive detention law would be applied. But in our Constitution no such specification is provided. As a result, this law has become the sharp weapon to suppress the political opponent of the government.

This is a sinister looking feature of a democratic constitution. This is undoubtedly unfortunate. The SPA has turned into a draconian law. Because–

(i) A detainee under this law has not been given any right, by appointing a lawyer, to know from a judicial body why has he been detained?

(ii) The government can arrest and detain any person at any time it wishes.

(iii) The government can, if wishes, detain a person for an indefinite period.

(iv) It is factually negating all the avowed commitment and spirit of the constitution and human rights.

On 7 September 2000 a three member Sub-committee of the Parliamentary Standing Committee submitted a 31 pages report on SPA to the Parliament. The Sub-committee mentioned that 69,010 people were detained under the controversial SPA of 1974 in the last 24 years and 68,195 persons detained under this Act were released by the order of the High Court Division.[61] After studying the verdicts in 100 cases the Sub-committee identified 16 reasons for which the court declared the detention illegal. These reasons included[62]:

(a) vague, indefinite and uncertain grounds for detention;
(b) governments unlawful authority in ordering detention;
(c) non-placement of grounds for detention within 120 days;
(d) lack of basis for detention order;
(e) for political reasons mixing of good grounds with bad one;
(f) failure to show reasons for detention within 15 days;
(g) government failure to produce necessary papers in court; and
(h) delayed government order for extension of detention.

Despite the findings of the said Sub-committee, the Parliament has recommended the retention of this repressive law, which is surprising to everybody.[63]

RIGHT TO SILENCE

Right to silence of a person accused of offence emanated from the common law jurisprudence that 'every person accused shall be presumed to be innocent unless found guilty by a competent court. Article 35(4) of the Constitution of Bangladesh says, "No person accused of any offence shall be compelled to be a witness against himself." Sections 25 and 26 of the Evidence Act, 1872 support the above view. Section 25 states "No confession made to a police officer shall be proved as against a person accused of any offence". Section 26 further states "No confession made by any person whilst he is in the custody of a police officer, unless it be made in the immediate presence of a Magistrate, shall be proved as against such person." Sections 342 and 343 of the Cr. P. C. protect the accused against making false statement or against refusal to answer, forbid administering oath upon him and prohibit influence of any kind to be exerted for disclosure of facts save as provided in Sections 337 and 338 of the Code tendering pardon to accomplice on condition of his making disclosure of facts etc.[64]

Again a plain reading of Sections 61 and 167 of the Cr. P. C. reveals that the police investigation of the offence in the case of a person arrested without warrant should be completed in the first instance within twenty-four hours under Section 61 or if not then within fifteen days under Section 167. Any Police Officer making an investigation may examine orally any person supposed to be acquainted with the facts and circumstances of the case. Section 161(2) provides that civilities should be followed by Police Officer when making oral examination. A person during oral examination shall be bound to answer all questions relating to the case put to him by the concerned Police Officer, other than these questions which would have a tendency to expose him to a criminal charge or to a penalty or forfeiture.[65] Any statement made to a Police Officer cannot be used for any purpose of any inquiry or trial in respect of any offence under investigation. This statement may be used to contradict such witness.[66] So any statement made to police is inadmissible in evidence under Section 162 of the Cr. P. C. and any confession made to a Police Officer is inadmissible under Sections 25 and 26 of the Evidence Act.[67]

Section 163 of the Code prohibits a Police Officer or any other person in authority from offering or making any inducement, threat or promise for making disclosure of facts having reference to the charge against him. From the above provisions, it is explicit that a confession made to a Police Officer is not admissible, but it can be used in evidence of the thing recovered as a result of the confession made to a Police Officer by the accused.[68] Thus if weapon used in a case is recovered by the police as a result of confession made by an accused person, the recovery is a relevant piece of evidence.[69]

A bare perusing of the laws set forth above suggests that any person accused of an offence is protected against making any disclosure of facts having bearing upon the accusation and against cruel or degrading treatment thereby providing with right to silence. In *Miranda vs. Arizona*[70] case the American Supreme Court opined that the suspect must be given four warnings before he is put in interrogation, namely, (a) you have a right to remain silent, (b) anything you say can be used against you in a court of law, (c) you have a right to presence of an attorney and (d) if you cannot afford an attorney, one will be appointed for you prior to questioning. Unless the warnings are given evidence collected through interrogation is not admitted in court. In other advanced democratic countries similar rules are followed so as to ensure rights of citizens and every other individual taken into custody.

From the aforesaid provisions it is obvious that any information which may be obtained or extorted by taking an accused on remand and by applying physical torture or torture through any other means, the same information can not be considered as evidence and can not be used against him. Despite the above safeguarding provisions for the accused in Bangladesh, they are compelled under police pressure to give such confession, which incriminate them. It's a clear violation of human rights of the accused. Question arises that in spite of these legal bars, why the police compel the suspect to confess through torture?

A recent incident in this regard is the compulsion of extorting confession from Shaibal Saha Partha who has been implicated for allegedly issuing death threats to Leader of the Opposition, Sheikh Hasina in e-mail. Partha gave a statement that four days before the FIR was filed against him, the police on 25 August 2004 called him to the *Cyber Cafe* where he had allegedly sent the e-mail threat from, whisked him away to an undisclosed place and kept him there blindfolded for four days. He added that the day the FIR was filed, i.e. on August 29, he was taken to Dhanmondi Police Station blindfolded and mentally tortured. He was offered financial inducements to confess his involvement in August 21 grenade attack, which was a clear violation of fundamental rights of an accused guaranteed under Article 35(4) of the Constitution of Bangladesh.[71] Through this the LEA wanted to prove that they were able to arrest the actual perpetrators of 21August 2004 grenade attack. It is a process of averting the responsibilities which they oathed to preserve. Through this way confession is frequently used as a tool to establish guilt of the accused.

When the prosecution prays for remand, often the courts grant the request. After the period of remand, the arrested persons make voluntary confession before a Magistrate though in circumstances beyond the visibility of police, in most of the cases the police physically produce him/her and will physically take him/her away in chains or ropes to the jail custody. Why should a person confess his guilt unless he is driven by conscience? Such persons are rarities. Ordinarily a person is tortured, coerced or intimidated in police custody. Subjected under such realities even an innocent person would tender confession if only to save him/herself from the assault. This anti-practice of the constitutional rights is being exercised frequently in our country.

RIGHT TO FREEDOM FROM TORTURE AND CRUEL, INHUMANE OR DEGRADING TREATMENT OR PUNISHMENT

In spite of constitutional guarantees of the right to be free from torture, inhuman, cruel and degrading punishment, both physical and psychological, torture by the police like beating with a stick or rifle butt, electric shocks, pouring hot water in the nose, use of bar fetters etc, are widely reported to be used in Bangladesh. In different international, regional and constitutional documents, this right of the accused has been preserved carefully. Mention may be made of these provisions in order to illustrate, the importance and significance of this inherent right of the persons accused.

Article 5 of the UDHR states, "No one shall be subjected to torture or to cruel, inhuman or degrading treatment or punishment." In the same language the ICCPR also supports the preservation of this right against any kind of torture or punishment.[72] The European Convention on Human Rights and Fundamental Freedoms holds the same opinion regarding this right.[73] It has been stated in the American Declaration, "Every individual who has been deprived of his liberty has the right to human treatment during the time he is in custody.[74]

Every person accused of an offence has the right not to receive cruel, infamous or unusual punishment.[75] Again, the American Convention states, "No one shall be subjected to torture or to cruel, inhuman or degrading punishment or treatment. All persons deprived of their liberty shall be treated with respect for the inherent dignity of the human person.[76] Another regional instrument on human rights, the African Charter on Human and People's Rights (ACHPR) is of opinion that all forms of exploitations and degradation of man, particularly torture, cruel, inhuman or degrading punishment or treatment shall be prohibited.[77] These are the important provisions of international and regional documents, which clearly expressed torture of any nature as prohibitive and condemnable and must be stopped in iron hand by the government, as this is the most important function of the government.

Convention Against Torture and other Cruel Inhuman or Degrading Treatment or Punishment[78] states that, "no person shall be subjected to torture or to cruel, inhuman, or degrading punishment or treatment". In this regard the constitutional provisions of some States may be quoted. Article 14(2) of the Constitution of Pakistan provides, "No person shall be subjected to torture for the purpose of extracting evidence.[79] Constitution of Bangladesh also states that, "No person shall be subjected to torture or to cruel, inhuman, or degrading punishment or treatment.[80] Article 29 of the Police Act, 1861[81] and Dhaka Metropolitan Police Ordinance, 1976 also speak against torture. In spite of constitutional provisions, torture especially by the police and jail authority has become a routine work. Almost everyday we come to know through dailies and human rights journals the sad incidents of torture, degrading punishment, and inhuman treatment by the LEA.

A recent example may be cited here to show how inhuman torture is exercised by the LEA. On the basis of a report published in various newspapers titled "Madrasah teacher died due to torture in RAB custody", ODHIKAR investigated the matter on spot with assistance from Academy for Educational Development (AED).[82] ODHIKAR found that M. Shah Newaz Titu (30) was brutally tortured to death by Rapid

Action Battalion (RAB) on 6 August 2004 at Choumohani area under Double Mooring thana in Chittagong. He was an Assistant Teacher of Ketua Islamia Dakhil Madrasah in Chandpur. It was learnt that on 2 August 2004, Shah Newaz came with his cousin Munir Hossain Talukdar to the residence of his another cousin Margina Begum at Choumohani, Agrabad, Chittagong. Eyewitnesses of the incident Saiful Alam and Khairul Alam Enam informed ODHIKAR that on 4 August 2004 Shah Newaz and his cousin Munir were going to have a bath after having tea from the nearby Manlama Restaurant. Suddenly RAB Officials came there with two vans and started beating them with a strong stick. That time Ziaul Alam Dipu, brother in law of Shah Newaz, came from his house and found that some plain cloth people with arms were beating Shah Newaz and Munir. Some of them were searching the cash boxes and other goods for want of arms. He tried to convince them and told them Shah Newaz and Munir were his relatives and came to Chittagong to visit his family. When he asked the RAB Official the reason of beating them, the RAB Officials got angry with him and tied him with his *gamcha* and started beating. Then they were taken to the yard of their house. At one stage some of the RAB personnel entered into the house of Ziaul Alam where they disarrayed the goods and furniture of his house while all members of that family were confined in their living room, other RAB personnel continued torture on the victims. Then they brought sofa from their house, forced Ziaul to sit on it and applied electric shock on him. They got the electric connection from the nearby storeroom and continuously gave shock to him, especially on the cracked skin and on the sexual organ.

After torturing them for three hours RAB took Zia in a CNG Taxi and Shah Newaz and Munir were taken by vans to an unknown place. At that time the physical condition of Shah Newaz was very bad. Muna, wife of Zia also complained that the RAB officials misbehaved with her. But RAB personnel did not find any kind of arms or ammunition from their house. On August 5 at around 5 o'clock in the morning, a phone call came from the Double Mooring Police Station to the house of

Zia's uncle and the caller informed that Zia and Munir were taken to the Police Station in a bad physical condition.

On hearing the news, Zia's uncle Saiful Alam, Zia's wife Muna and some other relations went to the police station together. A case under Section 19 (Cha) of the Arms Act was filed against the victims with the Double Mooring Police Station. Zia told his wife that he was tortured throughout the night; he had high temperature and could not stand or walk. After producing before the court they were taken to the jail custody. When his condition deteriorated he was shifted to the jail hospital. They were also informed that Shah Newaz was admitted in the Chittagong Medical College Hospital (CMCH) because of his deteriorated physical state. When his relatives reached there they found him unconscious. From the Medical Report it was revealed that he was suffering from injuries due to assault and succumbed to his injuries at 4.45 pm on 6 August 2004. Such types of inhuman torture were exercised by the RAB with these three victims but strangely there was no accountability of RAB. On the contrary, RAB Inspector M Ishaque filed a case under the Arms Act, 1878[83] against Ziaul Alam Dipu, Shah Newaz, and Munir Hossain Talukdar with the Double Mooring Police Station.

Another example of police brutality is the case of Sheema Chowdhury, a girl of 17 years and a Garment Factory worker in Chankbazar under Chittagong District. She was arrested by police on 8 October 1996 in the evening when she was walking with her fiance. She was taken to Rawjan thana where four police men raped her at mid-night after the OC left the Police Station. Sheema became unconscious as a result of rape. After medical examination, the doctor gave report of gang rape. Consequently she died in the hospital and she was burnt into ashes according to the rituals of Hindu religion, though she embraced Islam.

In 1997, 26 persons died in police and jail custody, out of whom 23 died in jail custody or under treatment of jail authorities and three in police custody, three persons lost their lives by police torture. Besides 28 persons were killed and 174 were injured by Police, BDR and ANSAR firing. Eleven women were raped by the members of the LEA.[84] But the actual figure is more than this because the unmarried girls and housewives do not report the incidents of rape for the sake of losing their prestige in the society.

Kalim Gazi of Shahpur, PS Keshabpur in Jessore District died of police torture like beating with rifle butts, kicking and blowing. He felt unconscious and on way to hospital he died on 13 November 1997. It was found after investigation that there was no case against Kalim Gazi. The only fault with him was that he protested against torture of his son, Hamidul had expressed his inability to pay bribe of Tk. 20,000.00 (twenty thousand) to the police. Another victim Nurul Absar, Night Guard of Fatikchari Thana Health Complex of Chittagong District died of police torture on 9 August, 1987 while he was in remand. Another victim of brutality was Mr. Nuruzzaman, an air crewman of Bangladesh Biman who died of police torture in Tejgaon Thana jail custody on 17 June 1997. His only fault was that he wished to ask the Prime Minister Sheikh Hasina about his fault for suspension. The incident created sensation among the conscious people that how brutal police torture snatched away the life of a strong and stout man who was suspended from his job.[85]

Abdus Sattar died by the torture of Fatulla Police Station of Narayongonj district on 19 May 1997. Police beat him by rifle butts and constantly kicked him in the belly. He died on the spot. But police told that he died of heart attack.[86]

In the above manner every year several incident of death take place due to police torture. It is not possible to mention all the incidents. From this any one can easily realise that how torture of the LEA are exercised in violating the constitutional safeguard in Article 35(5). Torture committed by Bangladesh Police in different times and in different techniques has been analysed by the Bangladesh Rehabilitation Centre for Trauma Victims (BRCT) from the reports received from different national dailies and newspapers. Significant among these are beating with sticks, kicking by boot-shoes, hurting with rifle butts, electric shock, bamboo pressure, putting of nails, pushing a needle in the hand, pouring hot water in the nose, throwing chilli in the eyes and mouth, pushing hot egg in the rectum; hitting the joints of the knees and under the feet, breaking fingers and nails, putting the head down and forcing one to drink urine etc. But the use of electric shock is found in all cases.[87]

VIOLATION OF RIGHTS OF THE ACCUSED

Fundamental human rights safeguards of the accused are being violated through various ways. The main LEA, police, at first arrests a person under Section 54 of the Cr. P. C, then takes him in remand under Section 167, violating Article 33 of Bangladesh Constitution, and at last tortures for extorting confession, violating Article 35(4) and 35(5) of the Constitution. This is the regular practice of the police.

A glaring example of such practice is the incident of Shamim Reza Rubel. Here the incident of police brutality is found in the killing of Rubel. On 23 July 1998, police of City Detective Branch of Dhaka arrested Rubel, a brilliant student of BBA, Independent University, near his house at about 4.30 pm. He was tortured barbarously in the Custody of Detective Branch (DB). As a result of physical and mental torture Rubel falsely said that he would give them firearms if he was allowed to go to his residence. After reaching near his house he withdrew his previous statement. Police then beat and kicked him mercilessly and threw him on electrical light post. Members of his family tried to save him from the claws of police, but failed. Rubel was taken to the custody of police again and he succumbed to death for their cruel and inhuman torture. The police claimed Tk. 200000.00 (two hundred thousand taka) as bribe on condition of Rubel's release; but Rubel's family didn't agree to that.[88] This incident exposes the ugly role of the police in protecting fundamental rights in Bangladesh. For this incident *BLAST, Ain O' Shalish Kendra (ASK), Sommilita Shamajik Andolon* and some other individuals filed a *writ petition* against some existing law by mean of which the police misuse their power. On this the High Court Division of the Supreme Court had taken an activist approach towards bringing the police back to compliance of law to safeguard the life and liberty of citizens. With that end in view Supreme Court had also provided a number of directives to be followed by police in matters of arrest and detention of suspects and humanising their treatment with the person in their custody.

In *BLAST vs. Bangladesh* a Division Bench of the High Court Division had made some recommendations for amendment of existing laws. The recommendations suggested regarding Sections 54 and 167 of the Cr. P. C. are mentioned below:[89]

Recommendation A(3)(b) on Section 54: A sub-section 2 shall be added to Section 54 which shall contain the following provisions, "Immediately after bringing the person arrested to the Police Station (PS), the Police Officer shall record the reasons for the arrest including the knowledge which he has about the involvement of the person in a cognisable offence, particulars of the offence, circumstance under which arrest was made, the source of information and the reasons for believing the information, description of the place, note the date and time of arrest, name and address of the person, if any, present at the time of arrest in a diary kept in the PS for that purpose".

Recommendation B(2)(b) on Section 167: Sub-section 2 of 167 be substituted by a new Sub-section 3 with the following provisions: "If no order for police custody is made under clause (c), the Investigating Officer shall interrogate the accused, if necessary, for the purpose of investigation, in a room specially made for the purpose with glass wall and grill in one side, within the view but not within hearing of a close relation of lawyer of the accused".

Recommendation B(2)(c) on Section 167: "If the Investigating Officer files any application to the court for taking any accused into custody for interrogation, he shall state in detail the grounds for taking the accused in custody and shall produce the case diary for consideration of the Magistrate. If the Magistrate is satisfied that the accused be sent back to police custody for a period not exceeding three days, after recording reasons, he may authorise detention in police custody for that period".

Recommendation B(2)(d) on Section 167: "Before passing an order under clause (c), the Magistrate shall ascertain whether the grounds for the arrest was furnished to the accused and the accused was given opportunity to consult lawyer of his choice, the Magistrate shall also hear the accused of his lawyer".

Recommendation B(3)(b) on Section 167: "If the order of the Magistrate is approved under clause (a), the accused, before he is taken in custody of the Investigating Officer, shall be examined by a doctor designated or by a Medical board constituted for the purpose and the report shall be submitted to the Magistrate concerned".

Recommendation B(3)(c) on Section 167: "After taking the accused in custody, only the Investigating Officer shall be entitled to interrogate the accused and after expiry of the period, the Investigating Officer shall produce him before the Magistrate. If the accused makes any allegation of any torture, the Magistrate shall at once send the accused to the same doctor or Medical board for examination'.

Recommendation B(3)(d) on Section 167: "If the Magistrate finds from the report of the doctor or Medical Board that the accused sustained injury during the period under police custody, he shall proceed under Section 190 (1)(c) of the Code against the Investigating Officer for committing offence under Section 330 of the Penal Code without filing of any petition of complaint by the accused".

Recommendation B(3)(e) on Section 167: "When any person dies in police custody or in jail, the Investigating Officer or the Jailor shall at once inform the nearest Magistrate of such death".

Recommendation C(1) on Section 167: "Existing Sub-section (2) be re-numbered as sub-section (3) and the following be added as sub-section (2)".

The same Division Bench also issued fifteen directions in this case to be henceforward followed by the police. The directions are as follows:[90]

No Police Officer shall arrest a person under Section 54 of the Cr. P. C. for the purpose of detaining him under Section 3 of the SPA.

A Police Officer shall disclose his identity and, if demanded, shall show his identity card to the person arrested and to the persons present at the time of arrest.

He shall record the reasons for the arrest and other particulars as mentioned in recommendation A(3)(b) in a separate register till a special diary is prescribed.

If he finds, any marks of injury on the person arrested, he shall record the reasons for such injury and shall take the person to nearest hospital or Government doctor for treatment and shall obtain a certificate from the attending doctor.

He shall furnish the reasons for arrest to person arrested within three hours of bringing him to the police station.

If the person is not arrested from his residence or place of business, he shall inform the nearest relation of the person over phone, if any, or through a messenger within one hour of bringing him to the police station.

He shall allow the person arrested to consult a lawyer of his choice if he so desires or to meet any of his nearest relations.

When such person is produced before the nearest Magistrate under Section 61, the Police Officer shall state in his forwarding letter under Section 167(1) of the Cr. P. C. as to why the investigation could not be completed within twenty-four hours, why he consider that the accusation or the information against that person is well-founded. He shall also transmit copy of the relevant entries in the case diary BP Form 38[91] to the same Magistrate.

If the Magistrate is satisfied on consideration of the reasons stated in the forwarding letter as to whether the accusation or the information is well founded and that there are materials in the case diary for detaining the person in custody, the Magistrate shall pass an order for further detention in jail. Otherwise, ha shall release the person forthwith.

If the Magistrate releases a person on the ground that the accusation or the information against the person produced before him is not well-founded and there are no materials in the case diary against that person, he shall proceed under Section 190(1)(c) of the Code against that Police Officer who arrested the person without warrant for committing offence under Section 220 of the Penal Code.

If the Magistrate passes an order for further detention in jail, the Investigating Officer shall interrogate the accused, if necessary, for the purpose of investigation in a room in the jail till the room as mentioned in recommendation B(2)(b) is constructed.

In the application for taking the accused in police custody for interrogation, the investigating officer shall state reasons as mentioned in recommendation B(2)(c).

If the Magistrate authorises detention in police custody, he shall follow the recommendations contained in recommendation B(2)(c) or Bs(d) and B(3)(b),(c) or (d) clauses.

The Police Officer of the police station who arrests a person under Section 54 or the Investigating Officer who takes a person in police custody or the jailor of the jail, as the case may be, shall at once inform the nearest Magistrate as recommended in recommendation B(3)(e) of the death of any person who dies in custody.

A Magistrate shall inquire into the death of a person in police custody or in jail as recommended in recommendation C(1) immediately after receiving information of such death.

In view of the above discussions, the Rule was disposed of with a direction upon the respondent Nos. 1 and 2 to implement the recommendations made therein within six months. All the respondents were also directed to implement the directions made above immediately.

After the High Court directive to amend Section 54 of the Cr. P. C the use of this provision had reduced to a large extent in the years 2003 and 2004. But the use of Sections 86 and 100 of Dhaka Metropolitan Police Ordinance[92] has increased. The police are using these two Sections as alternative to Section 54 in Dhaka city. It may be noted that actually there is no difference between Section 54 and Sections 86 and 100 of DMP Ord. The difference between Section 54 of the Cr. P. C. and Sections 86 and 100 of DMP Ord. is that Section 54 is applicable to the whole of Bangladesh while DMP Ord. is applicable to the Dhaka City only. During the period of September 2003 to May 2004, total number of arrests in Dhaka Metropolitan City was 69,715. Out of this number, 45,892 arrests were made under Sections 86 and 100 of the DMP Ord. and 4,360 arrests were made under Section 54 of the Cr. P. C. During this 11 months period 65.82 per cent of the total arrests were under Sections 86 and 100 of the DMP Ord. and 6.25 per cent of the total arrests were under Section 54 of the Cr. P. C. Thus DMP Police continued to use power of arbitrary arrest by switching from use of one legal provision to another.[93] It is found that police in Rajshahi, Khulna and Chittagong is abusing the law by arbitrary use of *Rajshahi Metropolitan Police Act* 1992, *Khulna Metropolitan Police Act* 1985 and *Chittagong Metropolitan Police Act* 1978 respectively. The statutes are almost same.

After the *BLAST* case in *Saifuzzaman vs. State*[94] another Division Bench of the High Court Division has taken serious notice of the flagrant violation of the fundamental rights of our citizens in the hand of the police and failure of the Magistrates in acting in accordance with law. While delivering the judgement of the court SK Sinha J. observed, "There are complaints about violation of human rights because of indiscriminate arrest of innocent persons by the LEA in exercising of power under Section 54 of the Cr. P. C. LEA put the people in preventive detention on prayer by the executive authority; and sometimes they are remanded to custody of the police by an order of the Magistrate under Section 167 of the Code and they are subjected to third degree methods[95] of torture with a view to extracting confession. This is termed by the Supreme Court of India as 'State terrorism' for which there is no answer to combat terrorism."[96]

His lordship issued eleven guidelines in more precise terms in the judgement of *Saifuzzaman's case* to be followed by the police and the Magistrates in matters of arrest, detention and remand of suspects and hoped that the requirements would curb the abusive power of the police and harassment of citizens in their custody. The issued guidelines are as follows:[97]

The Police Officer making the arrest of any person shall prepare a memorandum of arrest immediately after the arrest and such officer shall obtain the signature of the arrestee with the date and time of arrest in the said memorandum.

The Police Officer who arrested the person must intimate to a nearest relative of the arrestee and in the absence of the relative, to a friend to be suggested by the arrestee, as soon as practicable but not later than 6 (six) hours of such arrest notifying the time and place of arrest and the place of custody.

An entry must be made in the diary as to the ground of arrest and name of the person who informed the police to arrest the person or made the complaint along with his address and shall also disclose the names and particulars of the relative or the friend, as the case may be, to whom information is given about the arrest and the particulars of the Police Officer in whose custody the arrestee is staying.

Copies of all the documents including the memorandum of arrest, a copy of the information or complaint relating to the commission of cognisable offence and a copy of the entries in the diary should be sent to the Magistrate at the time of production of the arrestee for making the order of the Magistrate under section 167 of the Cr. P. C.

If the arrested person is taken on police remand, he must be produced before the Magistrate after the expiry of the period of such remand and in no case he shall be sent to the judicial custody after the period of such remand without producing him before the Magistrate.

Registration of a case against the arrested person is *sine-qua-non* for seeking the detention of the arrestee either to the police custody or in the judicial custody under Section 167(2) of the Code.

If a person is produced before a Magistrate with a prayer for his detention in any custody, without producing a copy of the entries in the diary as per item no. (IV) above, the Magistrate shall release him in accordance with Section 169 of the Cr. P. C. on taking a bond from him.

If a Police Officer seeks an arrested person to be shown arrested in a particular case who is already in custody, the Magistrate shall not allow such prayer unless the accused/ arrestee is produced before him with a copy of the entries in the diary relating to such case.

On the fulfilments of the above conditions, if the investigation of the case cannot be concluded within 15 days of the detention of the accused under Section 167(2), the Magistrate having jurisdiction to take cognisance of the case or with the prior permission of the judge or Tribunal having such power can send such accused person on remand under Section 344 of the Code for a term not exceeding 15 days at a time.

The Magistrate shall not make an order of detention of a person in the judicial custody if the police forwarding report disclose that the arrest has been made for the purpose of putting the arrestee in the preventive detention.

It shall be the duty of the Magistrate, before whom the accused person is produced, to satisfy that these requirements have been complied with before making any order relating to such accused under Section 167 of the Cr. P. C.

Saifuzzaman's case is an improvement to the BLAST case. In this case, as mentioned above, it was recommended that the date and time of the arrest will be put by the arrestee himself at the time of obtaining signature from him, the nearest relative or a friend of the arrestee must be intimated as soon as practicable but not latter than six hours, the Police Officer must make entry in the diary the name and address of the person who informed him to arrest the person; it is *sine-qua-non* (essential) to mention the case number in the case register for seeking detention. The Magistrate shall not allow an arrested person to be shown arrested in a particular case who is already in custody unless the accused is produce before him with a copy of the entries in diary relating to such case. If the investigation of the case cannot be concluded with fifteen days of the detention of the accused under Section 167(2) of the Cr. P. C., the Magistrate can send the accused person on remand under Section 344 of the Cr. P. C. for a term not exceeding fifteen days at a time.

In spite of having various directions of the court the human rights of the accused are not being preserved in accordance with the constitutional provisions. It is heard that for the protection of human rights an Independent Human Rights

Commission is going to be formed. An International Conference titled "Institutional Protection of Human Rights: Role of National Human Rights Institutions (NHRI)" organised jointly by the Law, Justice and Parliamentary Affairs Ministry, the United Nations Development Programme (UNDP) and the Australian High Commission was held from 19 to 21 September 2004 at the Dhaka Sheraton Hotel. This conference on institutional protection of human rights through national human rights institutions is the first of its kind in Bangladesh. In this conference the Law Minister in his speech said that the proposal for formation of an independent human rights commission is under the cabinet's consideration. He also added that all preconditions are there for establishment of the Commission and the sooner it is set up the better it is for the well being of the country and the citizens.[98] But the frustrating news is that Law Minister Moudud Ahmed recently said the government could not constitute the proposed commission due to non-co-operation of some ministers. The Bangladesh Nationalist Party (BNP) led Coalition Government had formed a Cabinet Committee headed by the Law Minister on 10 December in 2001 to prepare a draft bill for a National Human Rights Commission (NHC). The bill is gathering dust.[99] This is the human rights condition in Bangladesh.

CONSTITUTIONAL GUARANTEES OF THE WOMEN ACCUSED

The Constitution of Bangladesh contains some provisions relating to the rights of the accused either male or female. The Constitution provides that "all are equal before law and entitled to equal protection of law."[100] The implication of the term equality before law and equal protection of law is that nobody shall, on the grounds only of religion, race, caste, sex or place of birth be subjected to any disability, liability, restriction or condition. Equal treatment in the courts of law by the authority has been guaranteed to every citizens and non-citizens, male or female alike. Everyone has been endowed with the protection of law and it has been guaranteed that no action detrimental to the life, liberty, body, reputation or property of any person shall be taken except in accordance with law.[101] So, everybody is subject to same treatment regardless of sex in the eye of law.

Any body's life or personal liberty cannot be curtailed provided the provisions of law for the time being in force, which provide for such infringements.[102] Arrest and detention issues have been properly delineated in the said Constitution. It has also been said that every arrested person shall be communicated with the grounds of his/her arrest within twenty-four hours excluding the time necessary for the purpose of carrying the arrestee to the nearest Magistrate Court from the place of such arrest.[103] Every arrestee shall be provided with the facilities of the right to consult and be defended by a legal practitioner of his/her choice.[104] So, the accused irrespective of sex is on an equal footing, and entitled to such rights. These rights, guaranteed to an accused whether male or female, are not absolute and beyond any limitation. Any person who is arrested under the preventive detention order may be denied any of those rights.[105] An accused is not to be prosecuted and punished for the same offence more than once and it is equally applied to both male and female.[106] It is one of the fundamental rights of an accused to be punished for the commission of an offence which is a punishable offence under the law in force and he/she should not be subjected to a penalty greater than or different from, that which might have been inflicted under the law in force at the time of the commission of the offence.[107] Every accused either male or female enjoys the right to a speedy and public trial by an independent and impartial court or tribunal established by law.[108] No person accused of any offence is compelled to be a witness against him/herself[109] while no one is to be subjected to torture or to cruel, inhuman, or degrading punishment or treatment.[110]

CONCLUSION

Nothing that does not mutate or that is weighed down with inertia is sure to meet its inevitable end, sooner rather than latter. So mutation is must to serve for anything in this world. Law is not the exception; it must be changed with the changing needs of time. Sections 54 and 167 of the Cr. P. C. and some other legal provisions which help the executive authority to violate the fundamental rights of a citizen were enacted at the colonial period, for suppressing the native Indian, but now in this independent democratic Bangladesh how such a law can still be functioning while the Constitution guaranteed the fundamental rights to every citizen? That's the question. Moreover, we usually remark that a large number of people are being affected in police custody. In our country police custody means something menacing and ominously obscure. The family inmates of a young boy picked up by police can no longer forsee what was going to happen to the fate of the arrestee. The causes of such mistrust suffered by our LEA are so rooted into our socio-economic and political realities that a dependant policing cannot be effectively brought back on track unless variable police forces are built up in keeping with the changing needs of the time. So everywhere change is a must to protect the rights of the citizen as well as the rights of the accused. In such a situation the recommendations directed in *BLAST* and *Saifuzzaman's* cases are necessary to implement for preserving the rights of the accused. Again for an institutional protection of human rights the National Independent Human Rights Commission is essential to be established. It is expected that the government will take initiatives to protect human rights of the accused by considering the above legal provisions.

NOTES

1. M. Faiz-ud-Din, 'Human Rights and Constitutional Guarantees: Bangladesh Perspective', *The Islamic University Studies,* (Vol. 2 No. 1, 2000), Faculty of Law, Islamic University, Kushtia, 243.
2. *Constitution of Bangladesh,* Article 27.
3. M Faiz-ud-Din, *supra note* 1 at 245.
4. M. Faiz-ud-Din and M. Abdul Hannan, 'Protection of Human Rights in Criminal Justice: Bangladesh Perspective', *Research Project,* 1998, Rajshahi University, Bangladesh, 10.
5. *The Daily Inqilab,* Dhaka (Bangladesh), 20 July 1999. The website of the *Daily Inqilab* is: <http://*www.dailyinqilab.com*>
6. *Constitution of Bangladesh,* Article 32.

7. *International Covenant on Civil and Political Rights* 1966, Article 6.
8. *European Convention on Human Rights and Fundamental Freedoms (ECHR)*, Article 2.
9. *Ibid.*
10. *American Declaration of the Rights and Duties of Man (ADRDM)*, Article 1 .
11. *The American Convention on Human Rights (ACHR)* 1999.
12. *African Charter on Human and Peoples' Rights*, Article 4.
13. *Constitution of India*, Article 21.
14. *Constitution of Pakistan*, Article 9.
15. *Human Rights Fact Finder*, [Bangladesh Rehabilitation Centre for Trauma Victims (BRCT), March - April issues 1999].
16. *Human Rights Fact Finder*, (BRCT, January Issue 1998).
17. *The Daily Ittefaq*, Dhaka (Bangladesh), 1 January 1999 The website of the *Daily Ittefaq* is: *http://www.ittefaq.com*
18. *The Daily Inqilab*, Dhaka (Bangladesh), 26 June 1999. The website of the *Daily Inqilab* is: *http://www.dailyinqilab.com*
19. The *Daily Ittefaq*, Dhaka (Bangladesh), 27 December 2002 The website of the *Daily Ittefaq* is: *http://www.ittefaq.com*
20. *Ibid.*
21. *The Daily Star*, Dhaka (Bangladesh), 10 December 2004. The website of the *Daily Star* is: *http://www.thedailystar.net*
22. *Constitution of Bangladesh*, Article 33(1).
23. *Constitution of Bangladesh*, Article 33(2).
24. *Universal Declaration of Human Rights* 1948, Article 9.
25. *BLAST vs. Bangladesh*, 55 DLR 363.
26. (1968) 2 All ER 545.
27. *Babu Khan vs. State*, 55 DLR 547.
28. *The Legal Remembrance Manual* 1960, Rule 1 of Chapter XII.
29. *Code of Criminal Procedure* 1898, Section 340(1).
30. 36 DLR 333.
31. *Mobarak Ali (Md.) alias Mobarak Ali Mondal vs. Peoples Republic of Bangladesh* represented by the Ministry of Home Affairs, 50 DLR 10.

32. AIR 1954 (Raj) 241.
33. 27 Cr. L. J. 1169.
34. AIR 1951 (SC) 441.
35. AIR 1935 (Lah) 230.
36. AIR 1916 (Mad) 933.
37. *The State vs. Abdul Gazi,* 33 DLR 79.
38. *Abdul Gani vs. State,* 16 DLR 388.
39. *Abdul Mannan vs. The State,* 14 DLR 667.
40. *State vs.Robiul Hossain alias Rob,* 52 DLR (HCD) 370.
41. *Code of Criminal Procedure* 1898, Section 61.
42. *Abdur Rahman vs. State,* 29 DLR 256 (SC).
43. *Mehnaz Sakib vs. Bangladesh,* 52 DLR (HD) 526.
44. The word 'remand' is not defined in the codified law. The dictionary meaning of remand is to send back an accused to get further evidence. The term remand does not occur in Section 167 of the Cr. P. C. But in our country the police generally utilize this Section for the purpose of taking an accused person on remand. Though the provisions of Section 167 empower the Magistrate to authorise the detention in police custody, it is surprising to note that no guideline has been given in Sub-sections (2) and (3) as to the circumstances under which detention in police custody may be authorised.
45. Ahmad SM, *Police Regulations of Bengal, 1943,* (Kamrul Book House, Dhaka: 2003), 45.
46. *Annual Report 2002 of the BRCT,* Dhaka, 18.
47. *Annual Report 2003 of the BRCT,* Dhaka, 7.
48. *Hereinafter referred to as the* AB *or* the Board.
49. *Constitution of Bangladesh,* Article 33(4).
50. *Constitution of Bangladesh,* Article 33(5).
51. *The Special Powers Act* 1974, Section 3(2).
52. *The Special Powers Act* 1974, Section 3(3).
53. *The Special Powers Act* 1974, Section 8(1).
54. *The Special Powers Act* 1974, Section 8(2).
55. *The Special Powers Act* 1974, Section 10.
56. *The Special Powers Act* 1974, Section 11(1).

57. *Reita Rahman vs. Bangladesh,* 50 DLR 201.
58. *Zilaluddin vs. Bangladesh,* 54 DLR 625.
59. *The Special Powers Act* 1974, Section 2(f), and *see also* p. 45.
60. *Mokbul Hossain vs. Government of Bangladesh and Others,* 54 DLR 118.
61. *The Bangladesh Today,* Dhaka (Bangladesh), 19 February 2005.
62. *Ibid.*
63. *Ibid.*
64. *Code of Criminal Procedure* 1898, Sections 342, 343 and 337, 338; *See also* Chapter 4.5.
65. *Code of Criminal Procedure* 1898, Section 161(2).
66. *Code of Criminal Procedure* 1898, Section 162.
67. *Mohammad Siddiqur Rehman v. State,* 7 BLD (AD) 93.
68. *The Evidence Act 1872,* Section 27.
69. *State of UP vs. Deoman Upadhyaya,* AIR (1960) SC 1125.
70. *Minanda vs. Arizona,* 348 US 436.
71. *The Daily Star,* Dhaka (Bangladesh), 21 September 2004. The website of the *Daily Stat* is: <*http://www.thedailystar.net*>.
72. *International Covenant on Civil and Political Rights (ICCPR)* 1966, Article 7.
73. *European Convention on Human Rights and Fundamental Freedom (ECHRFF),* Article 3.
74. *American Declaration of the Rights and Duties of Man (ADRDM),* Article XXVI.
75. *Ibid.*
76. *American Convention on Human Rights,* Article 5(2).
77. *African Charter on Human and Peoples' Rights,* Article 5.
78. The Convention was adopted by the General Assembly of the UN in 1984 and was enforced in 1989.
79. *Constitution of Pakistan,* Article 14(2).
80. *Constitution of Bangladesh,* Article 35(5).
81. In 1861 this Act is enforced in Bangladesh.
82. *The Bangladesh Today,* Dhaka (Bangladesh), 4 September 2004.
83. Act No. XI of 1878.

84. *Human Rights Fact Finder,* (BRCT: March-April, 1997).
85. Ud-Din MF, and Hannan MA, *supra note* 4 at 29.
86. Ud-Din MF, *supra note* 1 at 258.
87. Annual Reports of BRCT 1997, *State of Human Rights,* 50.
88. Bangladesh Rehabilitation Centre for Trauma Victims (BRCT), Dhaka, *Annual Report* 1998, 8.
89. 55 DLR 373-378.
90. 55 DLR 380-381.
91. Bangladesh Police Form No. 38 regarding case diary.
92. *Hereinafter referred* to as DMP Ord.
93. "Human Rights and Police Custody: A perspective of Dhaka Metropolitan Police", written by Jesmul Hasan and Sazzad Hussain, It was presented at a Seminar on "Human Rights and Police Custody" organised by *ODHIKAR* and published in the *Bangladesh Today,* Dhaka (Bangladesh), 7 August 2004
94. *Saifuzzaman vs. State,* 56 DLR 324.
95. *See* Chapter 1.3.
96. *Ibid.*
97. 56 DLR 342-343.
98. *The Daily Star,* Dhaka (Bangladesh), 26 September 2004. The website of the *Daily Star* is: *http://www.thedailystar.net*
99. *The Daily Star,* Dhaka (Bangladesh), 10 December 2004. The website of the *Daily Star* is: *http://www.thedailystar.net*
100. *Constitution of Bangladesh,* Article 27.
101. *Constitution of Bangladesh,* Article 31.
102. *Constitution of Bangladesh,* Article 32.
103. *Constitution of Bangladesh,* Article 33(1).
104. *Constitution of Bangladesh,* Article 33(2).
105. *Ibid.*
106. *Constitution of Bangladesh,* Article 35(1).
107. *Constitution of Bangladesh,* Article 35(2).
108. *Constitution of Bangladesh,* Article 35(3).
109. *Constitution of Bangladesh,* Article 35(4).
110. *Constitution of Bangladesh,* Article 35(5).

ACCUSED PERSONS AND THE ROLE OF POLICE

3

INTRODUCTION

Criminal justice system has the obligation to protect human rights of arrested and detained persons, because arrested and detained persons are considered as innocent before conviction under the provision of law. The arbitrary arrest and detention are grave violations of human rights. Human rights of arrested and detained persons are of universal concern that cuts across major legal and political boundaries. This chapter seeks to correlate internationally and nationally protected human rights, which are applicable in the criminal process. The rights of arrested and detained persons with special reference to the state of preventive detention under the SPA including the role of police in Bangladesh are set forth in detail have been dealt with in this chapter. It highlights the role of police as the main LEA in the protection of human rights in Bangladesh.

RIGHTS OF ARRESTED AND DETAINED PERSONS

Arrest means apprehension of a person by legal authority resulting in deprivation of his liberty. The word "arrest" refers to the act of depriving personal liberty and generally covers the period up to the point where the person is brought before the competent authority. The word "detention" on the other hand, refers to the state of deprivation of liberty, regardless of whether this follows from an arrest (custody, pre-trial detention) a conviction (imprisonment), kidnapping or some other act.[1] Arbitrary arrest and detention are grave violations of human rights and hundreds of thousands of persons are victimised through arbitrary arrest in the world. The UN has focused its attention not only on the arrest and detention of the political opponents, but also on the arbitrary arrest of other persons, and prisoners' treatment. The UN demands from the member states to treat detainees with respect and dignity and condemns those countries, which do not follow the legal procedure in accordance with the provisions of Article 10, paragraph 1 of the ICCPR.

PERMISSIBLE DEPRIVATION OF LIBERTY

Article 9 of the ICCPR guarantees a broad right to liberty of person, which may be "deprived" only in the cases provided for by law. The requirement of lawfulness extends to cover all coercively forms of deprivation of liberty, including measures for the supervised education of minors[2] or for the protection of the mentally ill.[3] In most of the paragraphs,[4] two cases of deprivation of liberty are emphasized: "arrest" and "detention". In accordance with their ordinary meaning, both forms refer only to acts of State officials and do not cover the holding of mentally ill persons in a psychiatric care.[5] In addition to the general requirement of lawfulness, a further specific prohibition on arbitrariness applies in these two cases, which is aimed at the legislature and at executive organs especially, the police. In the case of *Hammel vs. Madagascar*, the HRC deemed detention prior to expulsion to be a deprivation of liberty.[6] The General Comment 8/16 of the HRC illustrates that the right to liberty of person has a relatively broad scope of applicability, and it has thus far not recognised any forms of permissible deprivation of liberty going beyond the cases of arrest and detention.

RIGHT TO BE INFORMED OF THE ACCUSATION

Every person who is arrested i.e., merely someone who is arrested or taken into custody on a criminal charge must be informed of the reasons. When an arrest is made pursuant to criminal justice, the person arrested must be promptly informed of the charges lodged against him/her.[7] Article 9(2) of the ICCPR contains two different rights of the accused, i.e., the accused shall be informed, at the time of arrest, of the reasons for his/her arrest and he/she shall be promptly informed of any charges against him/her. These rights relate only to the stage of arrest not to the state of detention.[8] Once the person concerned has been charged with a criminal act, he/she is to be informed pursuant to Article 14(3)(a) of the ICCPR, "To be informed promptly and in detail in a language which he understands of the nature and cause of the charge against him".[9] The right to be informed serves the legal interests of arrested persons concerned, and above all it is to put them in a position to make use of their right of *habeas corpus* pursuant to Article 9(4) of the ICCPR.[10]

Apart from safeguarding the rights of the accused against unlawful investigation, search, seizure and other coercive measures, the criminal laws of Bangladesh grant him/her the right to be informed of the grounds of his/her arrest.[11] This is a very important right, which has been framed in favour of the accused.

The criminal jurisprudential principle requires informing the grounds of his/her arrest of the accused. The Constitution of Bangladesh has given a status of a fundamental right to accused person *vide* Article 33(1) of the Constitution stating that "No person who is arrested shall be detained in custody without being informed, as soon as may be, the grounds of such arrest, nor shall he be denied the right to consult and be defended by a legal practitioner of his choice". Besides, arrested and detained person in custody shall be produced before the nearest Magistrate within a period of twenty-four hours of such arrest.[12] This Article conforms Article 9 of the UDHR which states–"No one shall be subjected to arbitrary arrest, detention or exile." Article 33 of Bangladesh Constitution was amended in 1973 and replaced in the present form. Article 33(3) (b) provides that 33(1) and (2) shall not be applicable to a person who is arrested or detained under any preventive detention law and to any foreign enemy. This arrest or detention cannot be challenged in any court except High

Court Division of the Supreme Court of Bangladesh, if arrested under the SPA.

The rationale behind this constitutional provision is to protect the rights of the accused:

> "... this safeguard is that on hearing the grounds of his/her arrest, the arrested person will be in a position to make an application for bail or move the High Court Division for a writ of *habeas corpus* This will also enable him to prepare his defence well in time and give him opportunity to meet the case against him".[13]

The right to be informed of the grounds of arrest is regarded as an inalienable right of the accused. Sections 50, 55 and 75 of the Cr. P. C. recognise the right of the accused to be informed about the grounds of his/her arrest in cases of arrest made under a warrant. In cases of arrest without a warrant under Section 54, the case is not protected by Sections 50, 55 and 75 or any other provision of the Code requiring the Magistrate to notify the grounds of arrest to the arrested person.

The right 'to be informed of the grounds of arrest and detention' as enshrined in Article 22(1) of the Constitution does not require the full disclosure to the public of all the facts giving rise to the crime and this right is considered as fundamental for safeguarding the personal liberty of an individual in all mature legal systems. The sixth amendment of the Constitution of the USA echoes similar provisions, which states, "In all criminal prosecutions, the accused shall enjoy the right... to be informed of the nature and cause of the accusation". In the USA, the police can arrest any person without a warrant only when the person commits a crime in the presence of the police or there exists the probability that the perpetrator might flee. In the Constitution special rights for person in custody and pre-trial detention have been framed for the safeguard of the accused.

SPECIAL RIGHTS FOR PERSONS IN CUSTODY AND PRE-TRIAL DETENTION

Article 9(3) of the ICCPR provides that anyone arrested or detained on a criminal charge has the right to be brought promptly before a judge or authorised judicial officer. The HRC considered the case of several Bolivians arrested and detained on suspicion of being *guerrilleros*. Military authorities held the group incommunicado for 44 days before their first hearing in a military court. The HRC found the 44 days detention violated their right under Article 9(3) to be brought promptly before a judge.[14]

Personal Scope of Applicability

Article 9(3) of the ICCPR speaks about persons who have been arrested or detained on a criminal charge. The discussions on paragraph 3 of Article 9 dealt mainly with the search for an appropriate formulation for the personal scope of application.[15] Article 5(3) of the European Convention of Human Rights (ECHR) refers to any person arrested or detained in accordance with the provisions of paragraph 1(c) of this Article, i.e., to persons suspected of having committed an offence or having planned to do so. In contrast to the opinion of the Committee of Experts of the Council of Europe, which considered Article 9 of the Covenant to have a more limited scope of application,[16] the historical background of this provision shows that great efforts were made in the HRC to come up with a formulation that would guarantee a personal scope of applicability analogous to that under the ECHR. Particularly noteworthy is that the earlier formulation, which related solely to criminal acts already committed,[17] was replaced with a broader one. The special rights in Article 9(3) refer only to persons who have been arrested or detained for the purposes of criminal justice, i.e., to persons in custody and to pre-trial detainees.[18]

Custody

Regardless of whether a person has been arrested on the basis of a court order or due to action taken directly by executive authorities he/she must be brought promptly before a judge or some officer authorised by law to exercise judicial power. The question has been left open by Article 9(3) of the ICCPR that, "Anyone arrested or detained on a criminal charge shall be brought promptly before a judge or other officer authorised by law to exercise judicial power and shall be entitled to trial". So, custody must end within a few days with either release or remitted by a judge to pre-trial detention.

Pre-trial Detention

Article 9(3) of the ICCPR refers in this context to a 'reasonable time'. Whether a time is appropriate can be evaluated only in the light of all circumstances of a given case; it begins with when arrest is made or pre-trial detention is imposed, and it ends, according to the English version, with prosecution or according to the French and Spanish versions, only with a court ruling as provided in Article 14(3)(c) 'without undue delay' within which prosecution is to be initiated or a ruling is to be made against an accused.

Article 9(3) also contains an indirect claim to release from pre-trial detention in exchange for bail or some other guarantee. This results from the principle that pre-trial detention is an exception, together with the authority to make release dependent on the necessary guarantees.[19] For example, in *Bolanos vs. Ecuador*, pre-trial detention exceeding five years is held to constitute unlawful detention in violation of Article 9 paragraphs 1 and 3.[20] The ICCPR recognizing the implications of pre-trial detention stipulates in Article 9(4) that anyone who is deprived of his liberty by arrest or detention shall have the right to a fair trial or court review which begins from the moment of detention.

Under the laws of Bangladesh apart from the constitutional guarantees contained in Article 32 prohibiting the deprivation of the liberty of a citizen except by procedure established by law. The procedure governing the pre-trial detention is regulated by the Cr. P. C., SPA, Evidence Act, 1872 and other criminal legislations.

RIGHT TO HABEAS CORPUS PROCEEDINGS

All persons who have been deprived of their liberty are regardless of the reasons entitled to a right to have the detention reviewed in court without delay and the state must justify the reasons for such detention. If the state fails to satisfy the court as to the lawfulness of the person's detention, the court will order his/her release. This procedure is known as *habeas corpus*. This right, which stems from the Anglo-American legal principle of *habeas corpus,* exists regardless of whether deprivation of liberty is unlawful. Article 9(4) of the ICCPR may thus be violated even when a person is lawfully detained. When deprivation of liberty is based on a court decision, in particular, pre-trial detention or imprisonment, the claim to remand proceedings is usually satisfied.[21] The true significance of the right to remand thus comes to light in the case of custody or other security measures or in preventive cases of deprivation of liberty beyond required measures for criminal justice, such as detention of vagrants, drug addicts, the mentally ill and aliens.[22]

The decision in remand proceedings relates exclusively to the lawfulness of deprivation of liberty. If the remand proceeding is not satisfied, the court must order the immediate release of the person concerned. The decision must be made 'without delay', i.e., usually within several weeks.[23] However, this time limit depends on the type of deprivation of liberty and on the circumstances of a given case.

In case of violation of the fundamental rights as set in part III of the Constitution of Bangladesh, Article 102 empowered by Article 44, any person whose right has been infringed can file a petition of a writ of *habeas corpus* in the High Court Division of the Supreme Court of Bangladesh for restoration of such right.

RIGHT TO THE REMEDY OF COMPENSATION

Article 9(5) of the ICCPR guarantees a claim to compensation to all persons who have been unlawfully deprived of their liberty of person. Victims of unlawful arrest or detention have the right to go to court and claim compensation under the guarantees of Article 9(5) of the ICCPR. This claim can be considered as a specific type of domestic remedy within the meaning of Article 2(3) relating to liberty of person[24] and which appears in the Constitutions of many countries. It is another way of making the police and military accountable for their actions. The HRC commented that, so far no violation of Article 9(5) of the ICCPR has taken place. In its final views in several communications, however, it has emphasized that the state concerned is, as a result of ascertained violations of other paragraphs in Article 9, obligated to grant compensation pursuant to paragraph 5.[25] In a number of other cases, it has made reference to the duty of compensation without expressly mentioning this provision.[26]

In a decision of July 1994, the HRC held that victims of gross human rights violations such as torture are entitled under Article 2(3)(a) of the ICCPR to *an effective remedy* which entails the obligation of the present democratic government to carry out official investigations, to identify the individual perpetrators and to grant compensation to the victims.

RIGHT TO BAIL

The right to bail, which is another very important right, created in favour of the accused "is one of the foremost recognized social defences under criminal laws of any civilized society".[27] The object contemplated by bail is to "produce the release of a person from legal custody, by undertaking that he/she shall appear at the time and place designated and submit him/herself to the jurisdiction and judgement of the court".[28] The Penal and Criminal Codes provide for two types of offences, bailable and non-bailable. Under Section 96 of the Cr. P. C. in Bangladesh bail is a matter of right for bailable offences and the person arrested must be informed of his right to bail.[29] In cases of bailable offences, the granting of bail is mandatory. Such a person shall be released on a bail bond with or without a surety immediately while he is in custody of the concerned officer after his/her arrest or when such a person appears or brought before the Court at any stage of the criminal proceedings.

In cases of non-bailable offences, the judge or the magistrate, at his discretion, examine the facts of the case, and the arguments put forward by both the prosecution and the defence counsels, considers and decides on the question of granting bail.[30] Granting of bail in the matter of non-bailable offences therefore rests on the discretionary power of a judge or magistrate after hearing the prosecution and the defence.

HUMAN RIGHTS AND PREVENTIVE DETENTION UNDER THE SPA, 1974

In the original Constitution of Bangladesh, which was enacted in 1972, there was no provision relating to special powers for preventive detention, proclamation of emergency and suspension of fundamental rights. Rather, rights to protection from arrest and rights against detention were guaranteed under Articles 31 and 32 of the Constitution. Though there were laws in different countries of the Indian subcontinent regarding preventive detention, the framers of the Constitution of Bangladesh carefully avoided such type of oppressive provision.[31] Originally Article 33 did not leave any scope for preventive detention. But in 1973, this Article was replaced by the Second Amendment under which a person can be arrested and detained.[32] So according to the above Amendment, the fundamental rights discussed earlier are not available to the persons arrested or detained under preventive detention. The laws relating to preventive detention are enacted subsequent to the Amendment of Article 33 of the Constitution.

The SPA that came into force on 9 February 1974 was the result of the amendment of Article 33 of the Constitution. Clause 3 of Article 33 specifically lays down that these safeguards as to arrest and detention under clause (1) and (2) will not be applicable in cases of persons who are enemy aliens or who are arrested and detained under any law providing for preventive detention *i.e.* under the SPA.

Abuses and Demerits of this Law

Since under this law a person can be detained up to six months without the approval of the Advisory Board and up to indefinite period with the approval of the Advisory Board, this has been indiscriminately termed as a black and repressive law. All the political parties, since the enactment of the law, describing it as a repressive law, have been demanding its repeal, but for 31 years from its enactment, nothing has been done for repealing such anti-humanitarian law under which many innocent men and women had been and are being detained mostly on political ground.

Detention is of two types under Constitutional law, (i) punitive detention and (ii) preventive detention. Punitive detention is imposed by a Court of law while preventive detention is imposed by executive authority i.e. by District Magistrate (DM) or Additional District Magistrate (ADM).

Punitive detention is given to a person for committing a crime or wrong but preventive detention is awarded for preventing the accused from committing prejudicial acts. Suspicion or reasonable possibility of the impending commission of prejudicial acts is sufficient for preventive detention. Section 3 of the SPA gives power to the executive authority to arrest and detain someone on the subjective satisfaction of the concerned executive officer. If the concerned officer is personally satisfied that there is sufficient cause of suspicion against any person of committing any of the acts prohibited by the SPA, he can give order for preventive detention. The Executive Officers may quite likely abuse the power and as such he is not free from controversy. He is not accountable to anyone for awarding preventive detention. Political leaders very often exert influence upon the Magistrate or Additional Magistrate and also on the police officers so that they exercise subjective satisfaction for detaining political opponents.[33] It is a hard reality that in most of the cases the Magistrates try to serve the vindictive desire of the ruling party.

Whatever may be the expressed purpose of this Act, the inner intention is to crush the opposition parties. So the power of the preventive detention under this Act has been greatly abused for the last 31 years, as the ruling parties have also acknowledged it. Hundreds and thousands of political leaders and workers have been and are being detained under this law for a long period without any trial. This law, in actual practice, negates all the avowed commitment and spirit of the Constitution, particularly the fundamental rights guaranteed by it.[34]

Rule of Law *vis-à-vis* Preventive Detention

The Act provides for indefinite periods of detention of different terms without effective safeguards. This arbitrary and malicious exercise of discretion of the government is grossly against the doctrine of rule of law. DM or ADM can initially issue detention order for 30 days. Later, it can be extended by the approval of the Government. In this respect, the Ministry of Home Affairs plays a vital role. Under this Act, the detainee is not produced in a Court to defend him/herself by any legal practitioner. This is a denial of the constitutional safeguards of arrested and detained person who is not produced, as per the provision of this Act, to the nearest Magistrate within 24 hours from the time of his arrest. So this Act has been described by Gazi Muhammad Shahjahan MP of Bangladesh Nationalist Party (BNP) as "a jungle law framed by the previous Awami League Government in 1974".[35]

In case of detention beyond the period of 6 months, the approval of the Advisory Board comprising of three persons-two persons qualified to be appointed as Supreme Court Judge and one Senior Government Officer is necessary. The detainee can only submit a representation to the Advisory Board against his detention. But it is a very lengthy process and as such the detainee cannot receive any relief. Under this Act, the detainee may be kept inside the jail for years together subject to the satisfaction of the Advisory Board, because there is no provision in the law for legal representation by the detainee to the Advisory Board and as such he remains in the prison for indefinite period without trial and without court proceedings. This Act does not provide any compensation in favour of the detainee in case of his wrongful detention. That is why this Act was regarded by Justice Abdur Rahman Chowdhuary as the "blackest law of the black laws".[36]

Judicial Relief

Under the SPA, an aggrieved person, on account of his/her preventive detention, can file an application of writ of *habeas corpus* under Article 102 of the Constitution in the High Court Division and 95% of such cases are declared by the High Court Division as illegal and framed unlawfully.[37] The judiciary has, in innumerable cases, acted as a "bulwark against illegal detention". Detainees have been released by orders of the High Court Division following the filing of writ of *habeas corpus* or the initiation of proceedings under Section 491 of the Cr. P. C. In the vast majority of such cases, the Court has found the grounds of detention to be vague, indefinite and lacking in material particulars.[38] But after release of the detainee on High Court Division order, in most of the cases he is detained again and so on and so forth.[39] In this way, the numbers of detainees always remain higher than the numbers of released persons. Besides, in many cases, the poor detainees cannot bear the expenses of the cost of writ petition. The lawyers of the Supreme Court ask for an exorbitant fee and they remain inside the jail for years and in some cases some detainees die during detention without knowing the 'offence' on account of which they were arrested and detained.[40]

Some Remarkable Cases under the SPA

A very recent case of detention will surely manifest the worst application of this Act. Azaduddin, Chairman of number 7 Char-Alexander Union Parishad, PS Ramgati of Laxmipur district and a freedom fighter, was arrested under the SPA in 1996. He was also earlier arrested and detained twice under this Act, in 1996. In the present case, a High Court Division Bench consisting of Kazi A T Monowaruddin J and Muhammad Zoinul Abedeen J declared the detention of Azaduddin as illegal and without lawful authority and ordered his immediate release.[41] He was arrested for political jealousy and rivalry. The High Court Division in the earlier cases also declared his detention as illegal. Each time he has been detained by the order of the Deputy Commissioner of Laxmipur District on the same grounds. The High Court Division, on 1September 1999, ordered not only release of Azaduddin but also ordered the DM to pay compensation personally to Azaduddin of Tk. 10,000.00 (ten thousand taka) to be deposited in the High Court Division within 30 days from the date of order and as because the said DM repeatedly detained the said Chairman on the same unreasonable grounds, the learned judges treated it as contempt of court, and the victim was allowed to file a suit of contempt of court against the said DM. The Court also ordered the Secretary of the Ministry of Home to make an enquiry about those executive officers who repeatedly ordered illegal detention in the country and to take action against them. The Government sought leave petition to the Appellate Division against the order of the High Court Division, but it was rejected.

The case of *Habiba Mahmud vs. Bangladesh*[42] involves detention under Section 8 of the SPA. It was held that 'grounds' of detention must include facts as well. It was also held that under the provision of Article 33(5) of the Constitution, the Government has the constitutional protection not to disclose anything in public interest. In such a case, the High Court Division will decide on the question of public interest privilege. The Court is to hold a balance between the public interest and the grounds of detention.

In the case of *Nasima Begum vs. Bangladesh*[43] it was held that if it is manifest from the petition for judicial review that the cause or manner of detention stands adequately explained and justified, then the respondent need not file an affidavit in opposition to it and may support the detention orally on the petition itself. But if the petition contains allegations of fact, which if unrefuted supports the petitioner's case for illegality of detention then the order will be invalid.

In the case of *Nasrin Kader Siddiqui vs. Bangladesh*[44] it was held that where a prisoner is in custody on the basis of an order of conviction, the onus of the respondent is discharged as soon as the return relating to the appellant's custody shows that there is an order of conviction justifying the custody. However the warrant of commitment issued by someone not authorised by law can hardly prove the conviction.

In *Farzana Huq vs. Bangladesh*[45] Sanaul Huq Niru[46] was arrested and detained first on 13 September 1987 under the SPA. His detention was challenged in the court[47] and the court declared the detention illegal and directed the release of detainee on 10 May 1988. But Niru was not released. Another fresh order of detention was served against him on 29 September 1988. Niru was not placed before the Advisory Board within the statutory period of 120 days. The High Court Division again declared the detention order illegal and directed his release. But Niru was not released; rather a fresh detention order for the third time was served and it was challenged by another writ petition.[48] Again the Court declared the detention illegal and directed the detainee's release. But even this time Niru was not released; rather a fresh detention order for the fourth time was issued. The matter came up before a Division Bench of the High Court Division.[49]

The Court said:

> "The least can be said is that the detaining authority is paying little regard to the order of the court. It is unfortunate that the authority which is obligated under Article 32 of the Constitution to protect the liberty of the citizens and further required under Article 112 thereof to act in aid of the courts order should flout the laws by resorting to authoritarian acts ... we are satisfied that the detention is illegal and the detainee shall be set at liberty forthwith."

In another case, 4 leading members of the Bangladesh Nationalist Party (BNP) in March 1997, were arrested and detained in which the High Court Division Bench ruled that the detention order under SPA of 1974, was illegal and ordered that each of them be awarded Tk. 100000.00 (one hundred thousand taka) as compensation[50]. Mrs Bilkish Akhtar Hossain filed a writ petition against the detention of her husband Dr. Khondokar Mosharrof Hossain, who was one of the 4 BNP leaders and was arrested under the SPA. Md. Mozammel Haque J and Md. Hasan Ameen J of the High Court Division of the Supreme Court of Bangladesh said in the judgement of *Bilkish Akhtar Hossain vs. Bangladesh* of *habeas corpus* writ case:[51]

> "To detain a person means to curtail his fundamental right of liberty, right of movement and right to speak. When without trial such fundamental rights guaranteed by the constitution are curtailed and invaded by the discretionary action of the detaining authority, the very next moment the aggrieved citizen is entitled to seek relief under the Constitution in view of the provision of Article 44 read with Article 102 of the constitution. Right to liberty, right to movement and right to freedom are so much valuable fundamental rights of each citizen that no authority can take it away without due course of law...In the instant case it appears that the detainee's rights of freedom of

> movement (Article 36), the right of freedom of assembly (Article-37) and right to protection of life and personal liberty (Article 32) as guaranteed by the constitution have been invaded by the detaining authority with malafide intention under the garb of the Special Powers Act ... Therefore, we assess such reasonable and rational lump-sum monetary compensation of Tk.1, 000,00.00 (Taka one hundred thousand only) to be paid by the Respondent Nos. 1 and 2 to the detainee considering the above reasons and sufferings of the detainee and his social position."

The repressive character of the SPA and the consequent sufferings of the detainees as a result of improper application of this Act and moreover the helplessness of the judicial authorities is seen from the findings of some of the cases disposed of by the Supreme Court of Bangladesh. In one case, the Appellate Division observed:[52]

> "We have accordingly no doubt that the framers of the Constitution intended to empower the High Court Division to pass appropriate order in the case of illegal or improper deprivation of liberty of person and the power to do so is not at fettered because of the absence of nomenclature of the nature of writ in the Constitution".

The following table will show the number of detainees arrested during 1990-1999 under the SPA and kept in jail for years together without trial:[53]

Year	*Total Number*	*Number of Released Persons through Writ of Habeas Corpus*
1990	4615	1099
1991	5302	1710
1992	6497	1594
1993	3669	1066
1994	2968	830
1995	4173	1805
1996	5413	3376
1997	4016	Not available
1998	6740	Not available
1999	6650	Not available

The following statistics show the number of cases filed, set aside and pending under the SPA[54] during 1994-1998.

Year	Case Filed	Case Set aside	Case Pending
1994	659	470	189
1995	198	176	22
1996	1623	1585	38
1997	1870	1822	48
1998	918	881	37

The foregoing discussion reveals that the SPA was enacted to repress the opposition political leaders. And ironically this Act had been used against the leaders and activists of Awami League, which framed this oppressive law in 1974 to annihilate opposition political parties' leaders and workers.[55] This law must be repealed in order to uphold the principle of democracy, which provides for free and fair involvement in politics and political opinion. There has been reckless criticism against this repressive law from its inception by the opposition political parties' leaders who became the victims of the oppressive law. So the immediate repeal of the tyrannical law is suggested in order to develop the democratic and congenial atmosphere where all people will enjoy fundamental human rights, like, freedom of opinion, freedom of movement and liberty, rights to life and person etc. without any discrimination as to sex, language, political opinion, religion etc.

WOMEN AS ARRESTED AND DETAINED PERSONS

A person may be imprisoned either as an arrested or detained one. Either male or female may fall into this category. The laws regarding arrest and detention are not similar. There exists a separate law to deal with each of the issues. In Bangladesh, the Cr. P. C. deals with the provisions regarding arrest. Chapter V of the said Code expresses the provisions of arrest in Bangladesh.[56] Under this chapter arrest may be made generally[57] and it may also be made without warrant.[58] Both male and female may be arrested under the provisions of this chapter. While arresting anybody under these provisions, "the Police Officer or person concerned making arrest has been empowered to make actual touch of the body of the person to be arrested".[59] In case of women accused touch would be made by the female police but the practice is different from existing law. The Police Officer or person concerned making the arrest has also been allowed to use all necessary means to ensure the arrest if the person to be arrested makes any endeavour or attempt to evade the arrest.[60] The Police Officer or person concerned making the arrest has also been empowered to cause the death of the person to be arrested in such situation if he/she is an accused of an offence punishable with death or with imprisonment for life.[61] Again a Police Officer has been empowered to arrest any person without an order from a Magistrate and without a warrant under the provision of Section 54 of the Cr. P. C.[62]

On the other hand detention is made following the provisions of the Constitution of Bangladesh. Article 33 of the said Constitution speaks of the provisions regarding detention of any person.[63] Under this law, any person whether male or female may be arrested and detained before committing any cognisable offence if reasonable apprehension exists in the mind of the authority that he/she may commit such offence if he/she is allowed to move freely.

Anyway, both male and female who have been arrested and detained both under general and special laws have some basic human rights. It is a common provision that the female prisoners should be separated from the male. Again, an arrested or detained woman who is pregnant should be given special care and attention. If a person is arrested under general law following the order of a Magistrate or without the order of a Magistrate, he/she would be placed before the Magistrate within twenty four hours excluding the time necessary for the journey from the place of arrest to the court of the Magistrate. He/she should be communicated with the grounds of such arrest.[64] But this right has been denied to a person who has been detained or arrested under any law providing for preventive detention.[65]

THE ROLE OF POLICE IN BANGLADESH

Crime is one of the most serious threats to the society in many countries including Bangladesh, which has been adversely affecting not only life and property of the people but also routine of economic activities and thereby undermining the economic, social and political stability. In fact, crime is opposite to peace and tranquillity. Development cannot take place in a state where crime has become rampant. So peace and development are interdependent. It is the prime duty of the Government to protect the life and property of the citizens and in this respect police plays a vital role as agent of the government by controlling crime. Police has to control the criminals. Public depends primarily upon the police for personal safety as well as the safety of their property. Actually, policemen's sworn duty is to enforce law and keeping their position neutral, which is, of course, rare phenomenon in developing societies. Because sometimes the police personnel are used as tools against the opposition political parties' leaders and activists. However, prevention and detection of crime and maintenance of public order and many other extraneous duties are to be discharged by the policemen.[66] There is no ambiguity that the police play a vital role in the protection of human rights along with other rights, which a citizen can claim as a human being. Police in many cases is to uphold the legislated laws designed to protect the rights of the people.

Police and their Activities

The Police Act, 1861 empower the police to act for prevention of crimes and protection of fundamental human rights. There is no denial of the fact that the police are one of the main Law Enforcing Agencies in Bangladesh and they play a vital role in the protection of human rights. But the whole responsibilities of maintaining human rights do not hang upon the police. The responsibilities also depends on the political commitment of the Government and to the criminal justice administration. In establishing rule of law the criminal justice system has to play its role and in that system police is only but a vital fraction.[67] The law provides sanction against the deviants from illegal activities detrimental to a healthy living. Police deals with the violators and apprehend them to produce before the court to prove their guilt. The courts hear evidence for and against, and, when convinced of the guilt of the violators of law beyond all reasonable doubt, award sentences of various terms as prescribed by law. Finally the correctional institution take them over and keep them segregated from the rest of the society primarily to refrain them from committing offence and secondly to give them opportunity to rectify themselves so that they may come out to lead their life as useful citizens.[68] Thus from the above discussion it is clear that in establishing rule of law and to prevent any type of encroachment on human rights, role of police is absolutely essential but not the sole factor.

Though the police are called the protector of human rights; unfortunately policemen are also involved in the violation of human rights. Death under police custody, rape, physical and mental torture, bribe taking, protections of terrorists are frequently caused by the police. Torture under police custody during remand has shaken the faith of the conscious citizens regarding police in Bangladesh. *The Daily Ittefaq* on 17 April 1999 published that, 40% crime in Dhaka City are committed directly or indirectly by the police. News items of the dailies reveal that not only in Dhaka but also in the whole country many grave violations of human rights have been committed by police and it is still prevailing.

Sheema Chowdhury of Chittagong became the victim of gang rape by 4 policemen and her death occurred in security custody in the jail during the period of investigation by police in 1996.[69] These four policemen who were involved in rape case were acquitted by the court because of defective investigation and destruction of symptoms. In 24 August of 1995 Yeasmin of Dinajpur became the victim of gang rape by police and after that she was killed by them. A case was filed in the Magistrate Court of Rangpur about this offence on 31 August 1997 where the Special Court of Rangpur gave death sentence to three accused police, Assistant Sub-inspector Moinul, constable Sattar and Patrol Car driver Ammrito Lal

Bormon. An appeal was filed in the High Court Division and later in the Appellate Division of the Bangladesh Supreme Court against the decision of the Rangpur Special Court, which was rejected in both the cases. The accused persons then submitted mercy petitions to the President under Article 49 of the Constitution of Bangladesh. But the President rejected those mercy petitions. Finally, after 9 years of the offence, the order of death sentence has been executed against all the three accused.[70] , In 1998 Tania, a girl of six years was raped by police in Control Room in Dhaka Chief Metropolitan Magistrate (CMM) Court area. In another incident Shamsuddin (Jewel) died at South Kamlapur near slum area of Dhaka on 15 November 1999. He was chased by police and he fell in a deep drain. He cried for help to save his life but the chasing police did not rescue him. Even they prevented other persons who came for his rescue. Bangladesh Rehabilitation Centre for Trauma Victims (BRCT) and Bangladesh Human Rights Bureau (BHRB) held a joint Press Conference at National Press Club on 24 November 1999 after their independent investigations that was published in almost all the dailies. Both the organization made spot investigation from 18 to 21 November and prepared a report and gave it to the journalists for publication. According to their statement, there was no definite case against Jewel. As per evidence from the eyewitnesses it was revealed that he fell into the deep drain as a result of police chasing. Police stood near the drain and did not rescue him though he cried for help and ultimately he died. Local witnesses identified the responsible police in the Motijheel Police Station through identification parade and four policemen were found responsible for the death of Jewel. Accordingly, a case was filed in the CMM Court against those policemen who were responsible for his death. This incident exposes the ugly role of the police in Bangladesh.[71]

Another incident of police brutality is found in the killing of Shamim Reza (Rubel).[72] Rubel was taken to the custody of police where he succumbed to death from their cruel and inhuman torture. One day *Hartal* was observed by the opposition political parties against the killing of Rubel.[73]

A report published in a renowned daily[74] describing the statistics relating to offences by the police from the years 1971 to 1996 can be summarised as follows:

Nature of Crime	*Number of complaints*	*Investigated steps taken*	*Punished*	*Remarks*
Torture, Bribery corruption, Torture of women etc.	90000	11923	2020	In most of the cases no investigation is done
Died in Police Custody	18911	321	3	
Rape and Torture under Trial	5867	112	-	19 cases are of women
Bribery, corruption and abuses of powers	50000	11000	-	Investigation was not properly done

Source: The Chittagong University of Law Journal, Vol. V, 2000,172.

Statistics of death, rape and torture under police custody and bullet injury by the member of other LEA are as follows:

Year	*Death under police custody*	*Torture by BDR, ANSAR & Police*	*Killed by Firing*	*Death in Jail Custody*	*Rape by Police, ANSAR & BDR*	*Bullet Injury by Police, BDR & ANSAR*
1994	12	3014	20	31	-	67
1995	12	2810	34	10	40	38
1996	19	3617	43	29	11	60
1997	04	3000	28	23	16	174
1998	16	555	26	52	21	74
1999	100	490	N/A	48	14	N/A
2000	106	518	N/A	56	36	N/A

Source: Human Rights Fact Finder & The Annual Report of Bangladesh Rehabilitation of Trauma Victims (BRCT) 1994-2000.

In the Annual Report of Amnesty International, 2001, it is disclosed that 50 peoples died in the police custody and the occurrence of rape in the police custody is frequently going on. On 26 February 2004 the USA Foreign Department has published its Annual Report, 2003 identifying Police as the main violator of human rights in Bangladesh. Remarkable features of this report are as follows:

- The police use excessive force to opposition political parties;
- The police use mental and physical torture during arrest and interrogation;
- The police easily get corrupt;
- Police are directly involved in woman and child trafficking;
- Police perform search without warrant in many cases;
- Punitive measures are being taken by police against journalists;
- Police and the Government Officials have committed rape to 31 victims;
- The number of death by police and other law enforcing agencies are 81;
- The number of death in jail and police custody is 113;
- The number of physically injured by police is 1296.

In view of the above findings it is observed that though the police has been entrusted as the custodian of law and order and with the noble duty of protecting public security but in practice they are appear as the misappropriating their powers and therefore causing violations to law and order. It has also been remarked that under Section 54 of the Cr. P. C. and Section 86 of the Dhaka Metropolitan Police Ordinance arrest, torture and death are taking a devastating form.[75] The police are violating human rights sometimes on their own initiative and sometimes by the influence of the government. Unexpected incidents are taking place frequently, which are destroying the holistic symbol of police as the protector of human rights.

The violation of human rights is mainly caused by police during the exercise of power under Sections 54 and 167 of the Cr. P. C. There are many articulations suggesting the amendment of Sections 54 and 167 of the Cr. P. C.[76] There is a glaring case in this respect, *BLAST vs. Bangladesh*[77] in which a modified form of Sections 54 and 167 of the Cr. P. C. has been prescribed. In this case it has been observed that,

> "We find that a good number of people died in the police custody after their arrest under Section 54 of the Cr. P. C. In 2002 number of custodial death is 38. This is absolutely shocking. Even the president of the country, in a speech delivered in 8th National Conference on Human Rights had to say that torture and inhuman treatment meted out to a person in custody and custodial death are against humanity and civilization. This speech was reported in the *Daily Ittefaq* on 27 December 2002 and also in other national dailies. Obviously, such tragic deaths resulted due to sweeping and unlaundered power given to a police officer under Section 54 of the Code. The power given to the police officer under this Section, in our view, to a large extent inconsistent with the provision of part III of the Constitution."

The court further said that the Government should make proper amendments of Section 54 of the Cr. P. C. to ensure the fundamental rights as guaranteed under Articles 27, 31, 32, 33 and 35 of the Constitution of Bangladesh.

During the period of 1972-1996 after the emergence of Bangladesh more than 90 thousand complaints were brought against police of which only 11923 complaints were investigated and 2020 policemen were sacked from their job; 18911 persons died under police custody by their torture; only 321 cases were lodged for such death and only 3 of them were disposed of. In the same period out of 5867 complaints of rape and torture against women by police, allegations were proved only against 112 policemen.[78]

Role of Police in International Arena

With the development of civilization the crime has taken an aggravated form due to the technical and communicational development. Criminals had made connection all over the world. In this situation it has become necessary to establish a close connection and co-operation among the countries of the world. With this view in 1923 a permanent structure for International Police Co-operation (INTERPOL) was set-up in Vienna. Bangladesh became a member of INTERPOL in 1988

Bangladesh delegate was elected as a member of the Executive Committee of INTERPOL in the General Assembly of INTERPOL held in Bangkok. As a member of the international community in 1989 a group of Bangladesh Police took part in Transition Assistance Group (UNTAG)[79] in Namibia under UN. In 1992 a group of 30 Police Officers took part in the UN Mission in Yugoslavia. Our police force also attended the UN Mission in Kampuchea. Participation of Bangladesh Police in peacekeeping operation in International arena has increased our reputation all over the world. In their behaviour, discipline and professional knowledge, Bangladesh Police showed an exemplary performance in its UN Mission and in fact gradually, they are being involved in various programmes of international importance.[80]

Police and Public Relations

The immorality, high handedness, rape, bribe taking are so common with the police in domestic sphere that each and every citizen of the country holds a very bad opinion against the police. Due to brutal behaviour of the maximum police personnel, their relation with the people is deteriorating in an alarming rate. But behaviour of police towards the public as has been provided in the Police Regulations of Bengal, 1943 (PRB) discloses the following:

No police force can work successfully, unless it wins the respect and good will of the public and secure its co-operation. All ranks, therefore while being firm in the execution of their duty, must show forbearance, civility and courtesy towards all classes, officers of superior rank must not only observe this instruction themselves but also on all occasions impress their subordinates with the necessity of causing as little friction as possible in the performance of their duties. Rudeness, harshness and brutality are forbidden; and every officer of superior rank must take immediate steps for the punishment of any offenders, which comes to his notices. Officers responsible for training a Probationary Assistant Superintendent shall impress upon him the necessity for showing courtesy towards gentlemen and teach him how to conduct himself towards them.[81]

The police powers were abused in the past mainly to stabilize the autocratic administration in the country. After the establishment of responsible government in the country, there has been a shift in the purpose of the police and a radical departure from the old practice to the new philosophy of service. Tradition has a great influence on practice, and in reality still there are thousands of complaints against the police, which should be avoided. The people used to consider policemen as dishonest, domineering and as the embodiment of evil. So instead of applying to police for aid and guidance in difficulty, people used to consider them lucky if they could remain away from them. But a contrary picture can be seen in many countries like Japan. In Japan there is a community police force named 'Koban', which is formed by a group of handsome and smiling men and women. Koban is a group of police who are well dressed, smiling and always ready to provide any assistance to the people. They help the old people and student to cross the road, to reach at home; they provide cash to the people who lost money.[82] That is the picture of police in most of the developed countries but in a developing country like Bangladesh, this type of police system is only a dream. It is desirable that the Bangladesh Police should come forward to remove this bad reputation. They must take necessary measures to restrain the miscreants, *mustans* and extortionist to ensure peaceful existence of both public and police. Expectation is that police force should no longer be isolated from the mass people; they should be a part of our daily life, our friends and guidance in difficulty.

But in course of time the trend of abuse of powers by police has not yet changed. Today the government uses the police as a weapon of dismantling their opponents. In addition to that police in order to extract bribe also abuses the powers. Besides, the miscreants influence police to abuse their power.

Corruption of Police

Annual Report 2002 of the Transparency International revealed that in Bangladesh police has obtained first position in respect of corruption. In that report it has mentioned some features of police, which are as follows:[83]

Ordinary people cannot submit FIR without giving money to police; almost 80% cases are filed by giving money and the amount of money may range from Tk. 500.00 to Tk. 50000.00;

The people face harassment during "Police Patrol" at night;

In many cases the police maintain relations with the criminals to collect their entertainment and transport cost from them.

The Weekly Khoborer Kagoj[84] on 7 April 2004 published that the amount of money, which are earned by police from the cases, are only 24% of their total illegal income. The amount of illegal money earned by police from cases are 25% and 30% in the District and Upazila levels respectively. In Metropolitan area 37% of total illegal money come from the illegal trades of drugs, firearms and from smuggling. The amount is 35% and 43% in the District and Upazila levels respectively. Police take monthly bribe from professional criminals and anti-socialists. The police take money from the disputant parties to arrest the opposite party, to taint the case or to make the bail easy, to exclude any name from the 'charge-sheet' etc.

In the Metropolitan area especially in Dhaka City *Chandabaji* of police is well known. Traffic and patrol police are taking money openly from the vehicles and temporary street shops. In Dhaka Metropolitan City in each shift 544 Traffic Police and sergeant work daily; they spend most of their time in collection of bribe. In Dhaka city there are 27 spots where the sergeants stop the vehicles to examine license and papers of the car. They collect Tk. 50.00 to Tk. 100.00 from every illegal license holders; in case of any fault in the necessary papers of the car the amount is bigger. At night, the police take bribe from commercial goods carriers.[85]

Some Problems in Police Force

There is no chance to deny that police are corrupted, they are torturer and in some cases fail to prevent crimes; but it is necessary to identify the reasons behind these. Lack of manpower, backdated firearms, lack of sufficient facilities i.e. transport system, communication, accommodation, low rationing; low-graded training; misuse of power by the government, inadequate travel facility, and absence of dearness allowances are the main obstacles to perform their duty properly. Nowadays criminals are well trained, carrying motor vehicles, mobile phone and on the other hand the police are suffering from deficiency of the basic needs, which results in the failure of prevention of crime.

The police are leading a miserable life for lack of sufficient facilities. The daily expenses are increasing day by day; but their salary is not increasing, it is too meagre to meet the daily expenses. Almost 90% police are getting Tk.3000.00 to Tk. 5000.00 as salary, which is not sufficient to meet their family expenses. They are getting Tk.1200.00 as ration allowance, Tk. 35.00 for washing and shaving. In maximum days of a month they have to work for more than 8 hours and sometimes 16 to 18 hours; in return they get Tk.400.00 only as overtime payment per month. The condition of accommodation is miserable in police camp. In most of the camp they have to sleep crowded on the floor. They don't get routine leave and have to stay away from their family, which results in mental pressure on them.[86]

The four-party alliance formed the government in October 2001. They gave priority for protection of terrorism and for this certain steps have been taken for modification and modernization of the police force; but the entire steps are holding on for lack of financial sanction. To increase the manpower the government has decided to form an "Armed Police Battalion" consisting of 771 members and has created 5768 new posts in the main force and 400 new posts for special branch. But the recruitment is not going on for lack of money.[87]

The total number of police post up to February 2004 was 109,953 of which 8636 are vacant. It may be mentioned that at present the ratio of police and population in our country is 1: 1350 compared to 1:585 in the USA; 1:560 in the UK; 1:728 in India and 1:625 in Pakistan. The proposition for new recruitment is not taking place for want of sanction.[88]

Due to the technological and communicational development, modern crime has taken an aggravated form. To prevent this modern form of crime Rapid Action Battalion (RAB) was formed of which 40% members have been taken from the army soldiers and 60% from the police. The RAB consists of 5277 members. At present two third of total number of police forces are using 303 riffles which were invented during Second World War. The Ministry of Home Affairs has submitted a proposition to change these weapons and to arm the police with modern firearms. The police force need 5413 motor vehicles but they have only 3465. To buy more 1994 vehicles Home Ministry demanded Tk. 121 crore but Finance Ministry has promised to give Tk. 80 crore which has not been sanctioned still now".[89]

There are a few police personnel who remain honest despite the various problems mentioned above. People show no sympathy to them and find only the fault of the police, due to the reckless behaviours of the majority of the police as discussed earlier. A major part of our society does not regard the police as human being. They think that police is only police, a peculiar being doing their business with crimes and criminals. The police must be provided with more facility along with training to be honest in public relations.

Abuse of Powers and Remedial Measures

In Bangladesh police functions on the basis of the Police Act, 1861, Cr. P. C, the Police Training Manual, and the Police Regulations of Bengal (PRB). In Bangladesh police misuse powers mostly under legal coverage. Under Sections 54, 167 and 344 of the Cr. P. C. and under Section 3 of the SPA police can arrest and recommend to the Magistrate for granting remand and detention. Section 54 of the Cr. P. C and Section 3 of the SPA give wide range of powers to the Police Officer to arrest a person without warrant from the Magistrate. Under the coverage of these Sections police arrest, beat and torture the suspected offenders. After taking into remand the police torture the suspected detenue to extract confession.

Under Section 54 of the Cr. P. C. the police can arrest any person in cognisable cases provided in respect of arrest the necessary requirement of responsibility to prevent misuse of powers are followed. Arrest under this Section is discretionary but it must be cautiously used. The Police Officer cannot arrest anybody he/she likes. When there is a bonafide belief on the part of the Police Officer that an offence has been committed or is about to be committed, only then the Police Officer can arrest the suspected person. This Section provides no physical or mental torture on the arrested person. But the practices is that some dishonest Police Officers torture physically and mentally and take bribe from the person arrested under Section 54 of the Cr. P. C. by intimidating to implicate him with serious offences. This is the tragedy of the role of police.

Section 167 of the Cr. P. C. provides that when any person is arrested and detained in custody and it appears that the investigation cannot be completed within the period of twenty-four hours and there are grounds for believing that the accusation or information is well founded, then on application of the OC the Magistrate can grant remand for not more than fifteen days. In remand the police torture the arrested person to make confessional statement, though the confession made by the arrestee during remand does not carry any legal value unless it is made in the presence of the Magistrates. Section 25 of the Evidence Act, 1872 states "No confession made to the Police Officer shall be proved as against a person accused of any offence". Similarly Section 26 of the same Act states "No confession made by any person whilst he is in the custody of a Police Officer, unless it be made in the immediate presence of a Magistrate, shall be proved as against such person".

- Again according to Section 164 of the Cr. P. C. -
- A confession shall not be made to a Police Officer;
- It must be made in the presence of the Magistrate;
- A Magistrate shall not record it unless he is upon inquiry from the person making it, satisfied that it is voluntary.[90]

Despite these legal bars, why do the police torture the suspects inhumanly? In this respect general saying is that, most of the suspected offenders are generally of immoral character and a few of them feel remorse to tell the truth. It is not possible to elicit any information or confession from them by behaving well because it is not granted that a murderer upon whom a death is hanging will tell the truth.

In these circumstances, in order to check abuse and misuse of power by the police the following steps should be taken by the government on an urgent basis:[91]

- The police should be held responsible to the civil administration at each and every administrative tire of the country by changing the present warrant of precedence and administrative set-up;
- The disputed Section 54 of the Cr. P. C. should be immediately amended by curtailing the arbitrary and whimsical power of arrest;
- Sections 167 and 344 of the Cr. P. C. are to be reviewed for modification, coping with constitutional provisions so that torture in the name of remand shall be up-rooted;
- A separate department should be created within the existing police exclusively for investigation of cases or complaints against police;
- The oppressive law of the SPA must be repealed immediately in order to stop the abuse of power both by Police Officer and ADM/ DM.
- With a view to stopping further gross miscarriage of justice all alleged homicide, rape and torture committed by police should be investigated and the responsible police should be tried and given exemplary punishment and the victims or their heirs should be given adequate compensation;
- Police are not to be used to SERVE the purpose of any political party, which has been clearly stated in the Police Regulations.
- Section 6 of the Police Code of Conduct, 1860 states that "the police shall discharge their duties neutrally". So the politicisation of the force must be stopped without undue delay;
- The proposed National Human Rights Commission (NHRC) should be established and given power to monitor and supervise the activities of the police and

to take strong disciplinary action in case of violation of any human rights or misuse of power;

- Honest and educated persons are to be appointed in police force and they are to be given training on human and fundamental rights along with moral and religious teaching.

Justice Kuldip Singh in his judgment in *D. K. Basu vs. State of West Bengal*[92] made the following recommendations to check the abuse of power by the police under Sections 54 and 167 of the Cr. P. C:

The police personnel carrying out the arrest and handling the interrogation of the arrestee should bear accurate visible nametags with their designations. The particulars of all such police personnel who handle interrogation of the arrestee must be recorded in the register.

The Police Officer carrying out the arrest of the arrestee shall prepare a memorandum of arrest and it shall be attested by at least one witness who may either be a member of the family of the arrestee or a respectable person of the locality from where the arrest is made. It shall also be countersigned by the arrestee and shall contain the time and date of arrest.

A person who has been arrested or detained and is being held in custody in a police station or interrogation centre or other lock up, shall be entitled to have one friend or relative or other person known to well being informed soon after arrest and of his detention at a particular place, unless the attesting witness of the memorandum of arrest is himself such a friend or a relative of the arrestee.

The time, place of arrest and name of custody of an arrested person must be notified by the police where the next friend or relative of such person lives outside the district or town through the legal aid organization in the district and the police station of the area concerned telegraphically within a period of 8 to 12 hours of the arrest.

The person arrested must be made aware of the right to have some one informed of his arrest or detention as soon as he is put under arrest or detention.

An entry must be made in the diary at the place of detention regarding the arrest of the person which shall also disclose the name of the next friend of the person who has been informed of the arrest and the names and particulars of the police officials in whose custody the arrestee is.

The arrestee should, where he/she so requests, be examined at the time of his arrest of any major and minor injuries, if any, present on his/her body and must be recorded at that time. The 'inspection memo' must be signed both by the arrestee and the Police Officer affecting the arrest and its copy must be provided to the arrestee.

The arrestee should be subjected to medical examination by a trained doctor every 48 hours during his detention in custody by a doctor on the panel of approved doctors appointed by the Director of Health Service of the state or territory concerned. Director of Health Services should prepare such a panel for all *tehsils* and districts.

Copies of all the documents including the 'memo of arrest' referred to above should be sent to the District Magistrate (DM) for his record.

The arrestee may be permitted to meet his lawyer during interrogation, though not throughout the interrogation.

A police control room should be provided at all district and state headquarters, where information regarding the arrest and the place of custody of the arrestee shall be communicated by the officer causing the arrest, within 12 hours of arrest and at the police control room it should be displayed on a conspicuous notice board.

If these measures are taken sincerely and honestly, violations of human rights by police will reduce remarkably.

Recommendations

In our country many steps of the police force remain ineffective due to political interference by the ruling party, interference by the 'Godfather' and some rich people of the society. Use of police force to serve political purposes has destroyed their morality. In respect of recruitment, promotion, transfer of police, favouritism and political consideration are playing a great role, which are creating chaos in police administration.

In the year 2003 'Centre for Strategic and Peace Studies'[93] had arranged a roundtable discussion in which the following recommendations had been made for the development of the police force:[94]

- There shall be a separate pay-scale in higher rate only for the police force;
- At the training period besides other curriculum importance has to be given on morality of the trainee;
- There shall be "Police intelligence" for the purpose of monitoring of police activities;
- In the recruitment political interference is to be avoided;
- There shall be a separate investigation department only for the investigation of the crimes committed by the police;
- Punishment should be increased in case of committing crimes committed by the police;
- Recruitment of Officer in-charge of a police station, Inspector and sub-inspector shall be made under Public Service Commission (PSC).
- Police shall be modernized with modern firearms, information technology and communication.
- Sections 54 and 167 of the Cr. P. C need to be changed as per the direction of the judgment of *BLAST vs. Bangladesh.*[95]

CONCLUSION

The foregoing discussions reveal that, it would be desirable to consider ways through which the right to a fair trial might be strengthened, for example, by making the right to a fair trial or certain aspects of the right non-derogable. In this regard, the study stresses on to consider the elaboration of a Third Optional Protocol to the ICCPR which would add in Article 14 of the ICCPR, i.e., the right to a fair trial provision, to the list of provisions which cannot be derogated from Article 4 of the Covenant. It is desirable to consider other means for strengthening the implementation of the right to a fair trial.

The Government of Bangladesh must pay attention to protect the rights of the accused, convicts and members of the Republic by taking necessary security measures against the violators, specially against law enforcing agencies by establishing more courts and appointing more judges for speedy and impartial trial. Importantly, Sections 54, 167 and 344 of the Cr. P. C. must be amended in order to stop torture committed by police in the name of "remand". Police very often misuse the application of Section 54 and maliciously arrest innocent persons in order to claim bribes from them. In the circumstances, effective and immediate actions are to be taken against these police officers, so that they and others cannot repeat such brutal activities in future. The study reveals that police is directly or indirectly responsible for committing major offences in the country. It is also revealed that the misapplication of the Special Powers Act 1974 is another cause for repression and illegal detention.

Apart from prevention and detection of crime and maintenance of public order, many other extraneous duties have been entrusted on police. They are overworked, underpaid, under manned and underestimated. However, a certain group of people claim that these peculiar being always seem to be around when they are not wanted and are impossible to find when desperately needed. With all the pitfalls and disillusions the policemen are found almost everywhere in the world on land, sea or the air, in hot or cold temperature. Whatever be the temperature or environment the policemen must always remain cool, courteous, impartial and it is imperative for the general people to offer whole hearted and unstained active support to help police to help themselves.[96]

We pray and hope that may Allah give good conscience to the police so that they can perform their duty properly in order to establish a violence free peaceful Bangladesh.

NOTES

1. The definition of "arrest" and "detention" contained in a study by the HRC in the early 1960s. For this distinction, *see* United

Nations, 'Study of the right of everyone to be free from arbitrary arrest, detention and exile', E/CN. 4/826/Res. 1.5 (New York: 1964). For this broad understanding of the term "detention", *see also* the mandate of the UN Working Group on Arbitrary Detention established recently by Human Rights Committee Res. *1991/42* and ECOSOC Res. *1991/42*. *See also*, Brody, 'The United Nations Creates a Working Group on Arbitrary Detention', *American Journal of International Law* (1991), 709

2. In the original proposals for an exhaustive listing of the cases of permissible deprivation of liberty, reference was made here not to "arrest" or " detention" but rather to the "parental or quasi-parental custody of minors" or to the "educational supervision of minors"; *see also*, Article 5(1)(d) of the ECHR.
3. General Comments 8/16 of the HRC, "The Committee points out that paragraph 1 is applicable to all deprivations of liberty, whether in criminal cases or in other cases such as, mental illness, vagrancy, drug addiction, educational purposes, immigration control, etc."
4. *International Covenant on Civil and Political Rights (ICCPR)* 1966, Paragraphs 1-5, Article 9.
5. Nowak M., *UN Covenant on Civil and Political Rights: CCPR Commentary*, (Kehl: Engel Publishers, 1993), 168.
6. No. 155/1983; see also, *VMRB vs. Canada*, No. 236/1987.
7. General Comment 8/16 of the HRC. It is true that some of the provisions of Article 9 (part of paragraph 2 and the whole of paragraph 3) are only applicable to persons against whom criminal charges are brought.
8. See, *Supra note* 1. Strangely, in this very case Article 7(4) of the ACHR aims only at detention.
9. Nowak M, *supra note* 5 at 174.
10. Distein, 'The Right to Life, Physical Integrity, and Liberty', in Henkin L (ed.) *The International Bill of Rights: The Covenant on Civil and Political Rights*, (New York: Columbia University Press, 1981), 131.
11. *The Code of Criminal Procedure* 1898, Section 56.
12. *Constitution of Bangladesh*, Article 33(2).
13. Nigam KK, 'Due Process of Law: A Comparative Study of Procedural Guarantees Against Deprivation of Personal Liberty

in the United States and India', 4 *Indian Journal of International Law* 99 (1962), 112.

14. *Lafuente Penarrieta et al. vs. Bolivia,* Selected decisions of the Human Rights Committee under the Optional Protocol, Vol. II, Communication No. *176/1984 (CCPR/C/OP/2), 1990.*
15. Bossuyt M. J., *Guide to the Travaux Preparatories of the International Covenant on Civil and Political Rights* (Dordrecht: Martinus Nijhoff Publishers, 1987), 207.
16. CE Doc. H(70)7, 29.
17. E/CN, 4/410: "Anyone arrested or detained on the charge of having committed a crime..."
18. Nowak M, *supra note* 5 at 176.
19. Muhammad N, 'Due Process of Law for Persons Accused of Crime', in Henkin L (ed.) *The International Bill of Rights: The Covenant on Civil and Political Rights,* (New York: Columbia University Press, 1981), at 138, 140; Holoubek, (1989) OZOR 105 at 143.
20. No. 238/1987, SS. 2.1. 8.3.9.
21. Dinstein, *supra note*10 at 134.
22. *See,* General Comments 8/16 of the Human Rights Committee.
23. Nowak M, *supra note* 5 at 179.
24. For the relationship between these two provisions see also *International Covenant on: Civil and Political Rights (ICCPR)* 1966, Article 2.
25. No. 9/1977; 132/1982.
26. *See,* e.g., No. 8/1977, at 13; *see also* de Zayas, Moller & Opsahl, 1985 GYBIL at 40.
27. Chaturveeli AN, *Rights of Accused under Indian Constitution,* (1984), 281.
28. *Black's Law Dictionary,* 4th Ed., 77.
29. *Code of Criminal Procedure* 1898, Section 50(2).
30. Khan MH, 'Effective Criminal Procedure and Judicial Strength', in Post-Editorial, *The Independent,* (Dhaka, 14 August 2000).
31. Ud-Din M. F. and Hannan M. A., 'Protection of Human Rights in Criminal Justice: Bangladesh Perspective', *Research Project,* 1998, (Rajshahi University, Bangladesh), 20; *see also* Chapter 1.3.

32. Article 33 has been substituted by Act XXIV of 1973, section for the original Article 33.
33. See, *The Dhaka Courier*, Dhaka (Bangladesh), 13 August 1999, pp. 16-17.
34. *Ibid.*
35. See, *The Daily Star*, Dhaka (Bangladesh), 25 July 1999. The website of the *Daily Star* is: <*http://www.thedailystar.net*>
36. Ud-Din MF, *Ayeen: Probandha Sankalon*, (Rajshahi: 1999), 152.
37. *The Dhaka Courier*, Dhaka (Bangladesh), 13 August 1999.
38. Khan AR, 'State of Human Rights: National Security Laws in Bangladesh', in *The Daily Star*, Dhaka (Bangladesh), 30 January 2000. The website of the Daily Star is: <*http://www.dailystar.net*>
39. See, *The Daily Star*, Dhaka (Bangladesh), 2 July 2000. The website of the Daily Star is: <*http://www.dailystar.net*>
40. See, *supra note* 36 at 42.
41. See, *The Daily Inqilab*, Dhaka (Bangladesh), 30 September 1999. The website of the *Daily Inqilab* is: <*http://www.dailyinqilab.com*>
42. 45 DLR (AD) 89.
43. 49 DLR (AD) 102.
44. 44 DLR (AD) 16.
45. 43 DLR 501, writ petition No 271 of 1990; *cited* in *The Daily Star*, Dhaka (Bangladesh), 25 July 1999. The website of the *Daily Star* is: <http:*//www.thedailystar.net*>.
46. *Hereinafter referred to as* Niru.
47. *Writ petition no.* 187 of 1988.
48. *Writ petition* No. 989 of 1989.
49. *Writ petition* No. 270 of 1990.
50. *Main Stream Law Reports (MLR)*, Vol. II, 1997, Dhaka (Bangladesh); *cited in The Daily Star*, Dhaka (Bangladesh), 30 January 2000. The website of the *Daily Star* is: <*http://www.thedailystar.net*>
51. 2 MLR (1997).
52. See, *The Daily Star*, Dhaka (Bangladesh), 25 July 1999. The website of the *Daily Star* is: <*http://www.thedailystar.net*>
53. Ministry of Home Affairs, *cited* in *The Dhaka Courier*, Dhaka (Bangladesh), 13 August 1999 and *The Daily Star*, Dhaka (Bangladesh), 25 July 1999.

54. See, *The Daily Sangbad,* Dhaka (Bangladesh), 21 October 1999.
55. See, *supra note* 36 at 153.
56. *Code of Criminal Procedure* 1898, Chapter V.
57. *Code of Criminal Procedure* 1898, Chapter V (A).
58. *Code of Criminal Procedure* 1898, Chapter V (B).
59. *Code of Criminal Procedure* 1898, Section 46(1).
60. *Code of Criminal Procedure* 1898, Section 46(2).
61. *Code of Criminal Procedure* 1898, Section 46(3).
62. Section 54 of the Cr. P. C. has mentioned earlier in Chapter 2.3.
63. *Constitution of Bangladesh,* Article 23(3).
64. *Constitution of Bangladesh,* Article 23(2).
65. *Constitution of Bangladesh,* Article 23(3)(b).
66. Haque E., 'Criminal Justice Administration Prerequisite, for Security and Freedom', in *Human Rights Law,* (Dhaka: 1997), 157.
67. Criminal justice system is comprised of the Codes (law), Constable (police), Court (magistrate) and Correction (jail). *See also,* Huq ME, *Criminal Justice System Administration,* (Ahsania Mission, Dhaka: 2001), 159.
68. *Ibid.*
69. *See also* Chapter 2.7.
70. *The Daily Prothom Alo,* Dhaka (Bangladesh), 1 & 2 September 2004. The website of the *Daily Prothom Alo* is: *<http://wwwprothom-alo.com>*
71. *The Daily Inqilab,* Dhaka (Bangladesh), 25 November 1999.
72. *See* Chapter 2.7.
73. *The Annual Report of BRCT* 1998, p. 8.
74. The *Daily Inqilab,* Dhaka (Bangladesh), 23 October 1996.
75. *The Daily Prothom Alo,* Dhaka (Bangladesh), 27 February 2004.
76. *See* Chapter 2.8.
77. *BLAST vs. Bangladesh,* 55 DLR 363.
78. Uddin MF, *supra note* 36 at 172.
79. A peacekeeping Mission of UN in Namibia.
80. Huq ME, *Criminal Justice System Administration: An Anthology,* (Ahsania Mission, Dhaka: 2001), 195.

81. Ahmad SM, *Police Regulations of Bengal,* 1943 (Dhaka: 2003), 22; *see also Police Regulations of Bengal* 1943, Section 33.

82. *The Daily Prothom Alo,* Dhaka (Bangladesh), 10 January 2004. The website of the *Daily Prothom Alo* is: <*http://www.prothom-alo.net*>

83. *The Weekly Khoborer Kagoj,* Dhaka (Bangladesh), 7 April 2004.

84. Since we have to prepare this research basing secondary sources namely journal, newspapers, weekly or reports covering differs issues we have to rely upon those sources. These can be treated as authentic.

85. *The Weekly Khoborer Kagoj,* Dhaka (Bangladesh), 7 April 2004.

86. *Ibid.*

87. *The Daily Prothom Alo,* Dhaka (Bangladesh), 7 April 2004. The website of the *Daily Prothom Alo* is: <*http://www.prothom-alo.net*>

88. Huq ME, *supra note* 81 at 16.

89. *The Daily Prothom Alo,* Dhaka (Bangladesh), 10 January 2004. The website of the *Daily Prothom Alo* is: <*http://www.prothom-alo.net*>

90. Huq Z, *Law and Practice of Criminal Procedure,* (Dhaka: 2001), 237.

91. Kabir AHM, 'Policing the Police', *The Daily Star,* Dhaka (Bangladesh), 2 August 1998. The website of the *Daily Star* is: <*http://www.dailystar.net*>.

92. AIR (SC) 610

93. A leading Non-governmental organisation in Bangladesh

94. *The Daily Prothom Alo,* Dhaka (Bangladesh), 10 January 2004. The website of the *Daily Prothom Alo* is: <*http://www.prothom-alo.net*>

95. 55 DLR 363.

96. Haque ME, *supra note* 81 at 26.

RIGHT TO REASONABLE INVESTIGATION PROCESS IN CRIMINAL JUSTICE 4

INTRODUCTION

Every prominent legal system of the world has reached to its development in a particular way in which human conduct and common human conscience played a very important role. The origin and development of administration of justice has its origin and development identical with the nature of human society in which they lived and their tendency towards the society. Human history shows man while leading a social life experienced conflict of interests, which paved the way for a developed machine of justice.[1] It further categorizes the conflict of interest into two categories; one is conflict of civil nature and the other is the conflict of public nature, while the latter was termed as crime.[2] Crime denotes to an act deemed by law as detrimental to the society at large. So criminal justice administration is intended to restrict those activities by punishing the wrongdoers through some particular procedure like investigation, interrogation, search and seizure of property. At the same time criminal justice system incorporates some rights to the wrongdoers regarding those procedures.

In this chapter a discussion have been made on the right to reasonable investigation, interrogation, search and seizure of property both in international and domestic perspective. Before entering into the discussion it will be relevant to have a short address of criminal legislation. In this respect it will not be erroneous to address the criminal legislation of the countries other than Bangladesh, because the legal system of the countries like India and Pakistan are almost similar. The legal system of UK and USA also deserves discussion in this respect, because all of them belong to the same legal family.[3]

CRIMINAL LEGISLATION

The criminal legislation of Bangladesh has a British colonial legacy, which at the outset of it was suppressive and exploitative in nature, and it does not suit presently in a country of democratic value. In our country we execute the criminal legislation through an institution called police authority. The criminal legislation confers on the police or investigating authority wide power in confiscating, investigating, inquiry and trial. Though it is said to be discretionary power there are limits within which they are to act. But the instance of criminal administration of justice in Bangladesh suggests that viles are being practised by the police authority and abuse of discretionary power is a regular practice in the country. In this context it will not be erroneous to say that in almost all the countries of the world police has been entrusted with the power of using discretion in searching the suspected place or person or premises and the seizure of property. But the core question concerning the discretionary power of police is whether the discretionary power is unbridled or subject to some administrative scrutiny? In case of Britain conferral of such power in search and seizure is subjected to reasonable grounds.[4]

Similarly, the criminal legislation of Bangladesh determines that the state machinery should involve the criminal process against offenders and also prescribes for securing a reasonable investigation, search and seizure. There are specific provisions regarding these, but some wrongs are being practised in applying these, every now and then. The LEA, like police in Bangladesh are placed in a position of great strain in that they are given a mandate of promoting social order, at the same time they should be circumscribed by variety of restrain as because governmental philosophy has transmitted from laissez fare to welfare. So those provisions should be noticed meticulously by the police in practice.

Criminal Investigation

An activity of the police on apprehension of criminals and detection of crime is criminal investigation.[5] The social engineers have emphatically advocated over this point of criminal investigation, because prompt apprehension of the criminals followed by their conviction strongly supported by investigation can result an appreciable reduction in the volume of crime. There are a lot of problems with the investigation procedure. For example the Bangladesh Police continues to hold the outmoded technique and procedure, lack of sophisticated method for detection of crime, insufficiency in communicative manner, and lack of enough manpower. A statistical report of *Daily Prothom Alo* suggest that in entire Bangladesh there are not so much police as New York City in USA has, said Hary K Tomas, the US Ambassador in Bangladesh, over a meeting while he was presiding.[6] This information envisages the necessity of enough manpower for upholding the investigation procedure and its efficiency. This is not the case with New York only. Almost all the developed countries have manpower involved in the criminal justice administration system.

One of the main objectives of criminal law is to protect the society by punishing offenders; at the same time justice and fair play require that no one should be convicted without a fair trial.[7] The primary object of the administration of justice should not only be done but also seen to have been done. Therefore, the administration of justice requires that every person accused of an offence is interrogated and searched in accordance with the procedure established by law so that when he/she is brought before the court for trial, and all the evidence collected against him is made available to the court for deciding as to prove his/her guilt or innocence.[8]

The criminal legislation of Bangladesh confers wide discretionary powers on the investigating authorities to make search and to seize things for the purpose of investigation, inquiry and trial. But the extent and the limit of these powers have been clearly defined by the lawmakers so that an accused is not subjected to unnecessary hardship and harassment at the hands of the investigating authorities. Yet the hardship suffered by the victims under police custody and unnecessary harassment by police have become a common phenomenon now a days. The success of police in ensuring clean and efficient criminal administration system has remained a matter of far away dream.

There are various reasons for this, e.g., because the police authority can not visit the place of occurrence at once both for technical insufficiency, scanty manpower and communication facilities which eventually results in pressure of work upon them. However if these situations could be changed the criminal justice administration system also would have been changed. Because now a days it is common that after the FIR the framing of charges takes a huge time, which results in encroachment of the basic human rights of arrested or detained, if not at least his right to freedom of movement or freedom of enjoyment of property. This lengthy process that results out of the problems mentioned above also have a negative impact upon the probative value of the case. The evidence either perishes or is found in a distorted form.

It is difficult to convict a man although it is certain that he has committed a crime. Because court evaluates the evidence before it that is procured by the police. Most of the time the police in our country produces the evidence in a mutilated form, so court is objectively bound to set the condemned free.[9] The police authority almost all the time is late to reach the spot, either for shortage of their manpower and viable instrument or for the scanty logistic support or any other reason.

Efficient investigation is neither a difficult nor an easy task. They should master the technique by which investigation is conducted and should be methodical in their work. Haphazard action and random thought should be discarded to make the criminal justice fruitful. Thus the investigator in arranging investigation must discover the exact moment when he can form a definite opinion. He may form preconceived opinion in reaching the conclusion unless he is forced to abandon it entirely. In this context it is said missing of true moment of forming charge-sheet amounts to a purposeless groping into the darkness.[10] The investigator shall take the case from the first stage with an open heart. He should have emphasised on the statement of the complaint. He will have to receive information from all quarters and his work at the investigating stage should be a great detail. He should make notes of everything and visit the place of occurrence etc. whichever an intelligent person thinks fit.

Initiation of Criminal Cases and Preliminary Investigation

The criminal legislation of Bangladesh suggests that a criminal case is initiated by the lodging of FIR under Section 154 of Cr. P. C. It provides, if any information in relation to any cognisable offence is brought to a Police Officer in-charge (OC) that shall be recorded in accordance with Section 154 of Cr. P. C. The FIR is the basis of any criminal case whether it is true of false, it highlights the intention of the informant, which was projected, to be set up by him at that time. The FIR should be meticulously recorded; it records circumstances before there is time for them to be forgotten. The report can be put in evidence.[11]

Though the FIR is not a substantive piece of evidence still it bears much value. Even the forms of FIR, which have been given under a circumstance of haste, should not be treated as an instrument of less value. The FIR should be distinguished from the information received after investigation, so the FIR should be apparent and of such nature that it creates some sort of encumbrance on police.

The FIR cannot be used for corroboration at the trial. It cannot be used for the conviction at the trial stage as because the FIR may also include within it some statements of confessional nature. It is merely a device of contradiction by prosecutor against the maker thereof, although a mere contradiction cannot be used as substantive evidence.[12] If the FIR is lodged by the accused himself even then it cannot be used as evidence against him at trial. That will be barred by Section 25 of the Evidence Act, 1872. If it is of confessional nature it cannot be proved against him. Where it is of non-confessional nature it is admissible in evidence as against the accused under Section 21 of the Evidence Act.

It is to be remembered that the FIR is the devise of setting the police in action.[13] So FIR should be immediate to the commencement of cognisable offence.[14] This rule is to protect manipulation and fabrication with the information. In case of information, which relates to a non-cognisable offence the investigating authority cannot initiate investigation without the approval of a Magistrate having competency and territorial jurisdiction. The Cr. P. C. does neither provide expressly any strict rules or directions to be complied with by the Magistrate in doing so nor the Cr. P. C. provides any manner in which the investigation should be carried out in a non-cognisable offence. A mandatory authority of such an order is implied in Section 155(2) of the Cr. P. C. Non-compliance of Section 155(2) may vitiate the ultimate proceedings and it has the probability of colliding with the constitutional provisions, at the same time the provision obliges the investigating authority to send the information of a non-cognisable offence to an empowered Magistrate for initiation of investigation process.[15]

The non-cognisable offences are generally of private nature. The police authority is under no responsibility to initiate the investigation into such cases unless ordered by a Magistrate. If in case of a non-cognisable offence police authority takes up investigation and finally submits a charge-sheet against the accused, and if the concerned Magistrate, being unaware of the provision of law, takes cognisance of the case and issues summon, the whole process is liable to be quashed.[16] Mere irregularity by an investigating officer not authorized to investigate a non-cognisable offence does not affect the legality of the proceedings of trial unless it is proved to be prejudicial to the accused and resulted in miscarriage of justice. The power to order investigation in non-cognisable cases can be implied from the mandatory provision laid down in Section 155(2) of the Cr. P. C. In case of non-cognisable offences non-compliance with the provision of Section 155(2) of the Cr. P. C. is immaterial.[17]

If we take the instances of modern developed countries that have been successful in carrying out an efficient criminal justice administration system we will find that most of them have categorised their crime. They have the specificity regarding their investigation rules. For example Russia being a member of the socialist law family it has developed separate and efficient form of criminal justice administration system. It will not be irrelevant to discuss about their system. In which if some sort of illegality is found the order of re-investigation is issued by the court and they are made subject to some sort of legal sanctions.[18] The statute lays down a period within which the organs, the investigating authorities are to investigate and collect evidence. There are some minute descriptions about the ways in which the investigation should continue. The rights and duties of the organs, and the methods are also specified.

But the activity of inquiry by the investigating organ depends upon whether the case requiring investigation is obligatory or not. The inquiry organ initiates the criminal proceedings and they are governed by criminal procedure.[19] In this case the outmoded police of our country is a total failure.[20]

But if we look at the modern developed countries of the world, which are successful in carrying out and settling a suitable criminal justice system, we will find that they have categorized the investigation process in a planned way. They have different sorts of investigation system for different types of crimes. For instance we take the investigation system of Russian. They have investigating system for grave crimes by the investigating authority named procurator, which is different from the authority that investigates in minor offences and is usually carried out by the militia units.[21] Though they are different bodies but their activities are carried on by the rules common or single, but they all are subordinated to one superior authority.

This is not the case of Russia only; almost all the developed countries of the world have adopted sophisticated strategies to cope with sophisticated crimes. Similarly the other common law countries also have structuralized their criminal justice system, which serves both the interest of public by punishing the criminal and the interest of the suspects. For example in England and Wales there are 43 police forces. Each are responsible for their respective areas but they are maintained and provided with resources by central and local government agencies under the supervision of local county committee and Magistrate, whereas, the Metropolitan Police Force is directly accountable to the government. The British Criminal Administration of Justice is such that it transpires the process in which the police are to act to defy the crime and at the same time abuse of power is prevented because of some legal obligations, e.g., accountability to County Committee on matters of efficiency, preparation of an annual report of the force concerned, seniority of the police is approved by the Home Secretary etc. upon the activities of police.[22] But unlike the developed worlds such change have not yet been introduced in our sub-continental countries. Investigation is still now either a hard job or sometimes violative of the human rights owing to the inadequacy of faculty and standard morality in the police. Degraded form of ethical values and unresponsiveness are also liable for these deficiencies. The police carry out the urgent acts of investigation to establish record of crimes along with inspection, search, seizure, interrogation and such other matters.

In Bangladesh the police perform the functions related with the investigation. The police have been performing the investigative work admirably, but with an outmoded way and procedure. In particular owing to the infra structural under developed condition in the rural areas, the movement of the police gets slow and they cannot reach the place of occurrence at once. The lapse of measures causes the destruction of the *alamat* of offence. Sometimes owing to the lack of manpower the police are incapable of communicating with the place of occurrence, which results in destruction of circumstantial evidence and eventually frustrates justice. Recently the socio-economic condition and degraded form of morality of police entices them to be relaxed in their investigative actions. Some practices of bribes have become a tradition in this respect.

In urban areas the police is a little bit fast. The practicality is that the entire process is boiled down in a stage of investigation by the Police Officer in the place of occurrence by confining the examination to some witnesses only. In cities the form of offences has a diversant nature. The forms and the manner sometimes are so sophisticated that the outmoded police authority owing to the lack of logistic support and proper training cannot cope with and excavate the truth of the fact.

Problems with the FIR

The FIR is the starting point of any case, on the basis of which the Sub-inspector being entrusted with responsibility goes to the place of occurrence. The FIR should be taken very meticulously. The source of information may be hesitant at the time of giving the information. The Officer in-charge should question the source. The Police Officer who is recording the first information and who is carrying on investigation should remain composed and try to set the best question to make the information out from the sources by intelligent questioning or interrogation. It suggests that the FIR should be well composed and should be added or omitted. It should not be deemed to be the brief or gist of the case or framework around which the case has to be build-up.

The FIR is not of the nature of a charge. It should suggest whether the case, which it concerns, is a cognisable or non-cognisable case. If in a case of non-cognisable offence the police inadvertently investigate about the matter without seeking any permission from the authorised officers, then such investigation by police will clearly encroach the rights guaranteed under Article 31 of the Constitution of Bangladesh since the non-cognisable offences are committed against a private individual. However, Section 155 of the Cr. P. C. does not intend to preclude the police from investigation upon those matters, what it requires is the maintenance of due process for ensuring justice.

RIGHT TO SILENCE

The right to silence is a constitutional right and belongs to the essence of a fair trial. But pertinently it is an inalienable right which requires to be provided to a person accused of an offence for ensuring his/her human rights. It refers to prohibition of use of direct or indirect physical or psychological pressure upon that person. In the modern humanitarian aspect the use of pressure ranging from torture to inordinate judicial sanctions to compel a person to testify against him/her is prohibited. This right of the accused is engrafted in Article 35(4) of the Constitution of Bangladesh. Article 35(4) states that, "No person accused of any offence shall be compelled to be a witness against himself". This is not the case in Bangladesh only. Almost all the countries of the world have inserted such provision within their respective constitutional system both on humanitarian grounds and for the establishment of fair trial. Again the criminal legislations of different countries also contain this right to keep silent to testify against himself.

The rationale that lies behind insertion of such right both in the Constitution and statute has been better explained by Sir Stephen in the following manner:

> "In the present day the rule that a man is presumed to be innocent till he is proved guilty is carried out in all its consequence. The plea of not guilty puts everything in issue, and the prosecutor has to prove everything that he alleges from the beginning. ... If it be asked why an accused person is presumed innocent ... the true answer is, not that the presumption is probably true, but that society in the present day is so much stronger than the individual, and is capable of inflicting so very much more harm on the individual than individual as a rule can inflict upon society, that it can afford to be generous".[23]

Such person shall not be compelled to answer those questions, which have the tendency to incriminate him as a wrong doer. However, the accused is allowed to keep his lip sealed placing his reliance on the rule of presumption of silence.[24] The rule giving protection against self-incrimination or in an oblique way right to silence has its root deep in Article 35(4) of the Constitution of Bangladesh. This constitutional provision can be interpreted to have some aspects, first of all its a right pertaining to a person accused of an offence, secondly, protection against compulsion to be a witness, thirdly, protection against such compulsion resulting in his giving evidence. The accused cannot be convicted of his involuntary confession extorted from him by the police by use of force.

The reasonable interpretation of Article 35(4) will unequivocally disclose the right of any person having right to fair and reasonable questioning and freedom from unfair extraction of information by the police. Which may otherwise mean right to silence is ensured in case of questions of incriminatory nature. Under the provision of Cr. P. C. the accused is obliged to respect investigation but he/she has a right not to incriminate him/herself. He/she is not bound to confer any guilt upon him/her and is entitled to keep his/her lips sealed placing his/her reliance on the presumption of innocence. This applies in case of such circumstances, which have reasonable prospect of exposing him/her to guilt. But if malpractice is done in the investigation procedure and information is extracted by applying the third degree method[25] then the court will be reluctant in giving any evidential value to this sort of confessions.

Since in the Sub-continental countries policemen are infamous for their double-edged attitude they often try to implicate the accused within a criminal charge which is far wider than the actual exposure to a charge. An instance of it in the case of *Nandini vs. Satiapathy*[26] the Supreme Court of India had sought to make police more sensitive towards human rights of the accused.[27]

However it is an established principle of law that the accused has the right not to give evidence against his/her defence. He has the right to remain silent while he is being interrogated by the police. But there may arise a very pertinent question as to what extent this right of the accused will extend. In *Nandini's* case it was held by the Indian Supreme Court that this right extends up to the earning of any evidence which if it were oral evidence would be protected; but this protection or right to keep off the lips of the accused does not cover the production of documents which does not contain any evidence prospecting to expose him/her to guilt. Productions of documents or being a witness are to separate things as has been stated in Section 139 of the Evidence Act, 1872. Section 139 states that persons summoned to produce document cannot be said to have become a witness by the mere fact of his production of document.[28] In view of Section 139 of the Evidence Act the Indian Supreme Court opines that every positive act of violating nature having the tendency of furnishing evidence is a testimony, which connotes coercion and procures the positive violation of evidentiary acts of the person as opposed to the negative attitude of silence or submission on his part.[29] Supreme Court of Bangladesh in dealing with the matter of Section 139 of the Evidence Act followed the principles pronounced by the Indian Supreme court.[30]

Therefore the phrase used in Article 35(4) of the Constitution of Bangladesh 'to be a witness' requires meticulous scrutiny which unequivocally reveals that the protection is not only available against the testimonial compulsion but also permeates even to the testimony obtained with priority. This right also extends to a person against whom charge of criminal offence has been brought, which in the normal course of it results in his prosecution.

BANGLADESH PERSPECTIVE

It is a common principle of criminal jurisprudence that the prosecution has to prove its case and the accused cannot be compelled to open his lips against himself. The rationale behind this principle in Bangladesh is that if the person accused is not safeguarded against self-incrimination he/she would be exposed to force, coercion and torture. The Constitution makers of Bangladesh also incorporated the same rule prohibiting the self-incrimination and have therefore given a constitutional defence under Article 35(4). In this context the rule against self-incrimination as depicted in the Constitution of Bangladesh resembles to this principle of rule against self-incrimination as embodied in the Constitution of USA, which later on was enunciated by the Fifth Amendment of that country. This rule was adopted in order to prevent the laws, which have the tendency to inflict harm upon individual and the society.[31] The history of criminal justice administration system suggests that in ancient time the accused was presumed to be guilty, so that the burden of proof of his innocence solely lied upon him. But in course of time when in countries where common law principle was established the principle of presumption of guilt of the accused was replaced by the presumption of innocence. The old concept became obsolete but still in many continental countries their criminal justice administration system is run on the basis of presumption of guilt of the accused.[32]

The rule against self-incrimination has been embodied in Article 35(4) of the Constitution of Bangladesh and Article 20(3) of the Constitution of India. This rule in Article 35(4) of the Constitution of Bangladesh is the composition of the following components: (a) Right pertaining to a person accused of an offence; (b) It is a protection against compulsion to be a witness in his/her own case; (c) It is a protection against such person resulting in his giving evidence. At the same time Section 161(1) of the Cr. P. C. provides that any empowered Police Officer may examine any person while investigating if he thought that the person proposed to be inquired has acquaintance with the projected offence. At the same time safeguards have been provided to the accused under Section 161(2) of the Cr. P. C.

Since the right to silence which in other words can be termed as the right not to be compelled to testify against own self is a human right protected under Article 14(3)(g) of the ICCPR. So it will not be irrelevant to discuss over the topic in the context of countries like UK, USA and India which will help us in identifying the purview of this right. USA as a member of one of the major common law system has introduced this right to silence or prohibition against self-incrimination by the accused through different cases and they have broadened the ambit of this right by the fifth amendment of their constitution. The Fifth Amendment provides, "No person shall be compelled in any criminal case to be a witness against himself".

Further the American court extended the privileges to the witnesses. In the case of *Counselman vs. Hitchcock*[33] the Supreme Court of USA said that, Section 132 of the Evidence Act of USA provides that an answer, which the witness is compelled to give, shall not subject him to any arrest or prosecution or be proved against him in any criminal proceedings and this protection is not confined to court room only it extends its purview to all governmental proceedings also.[34]

Notably this provision of Section 132 of Evidence Act of USA resembles to the proviso of Section 132 of Evidence Act 1872 of Bangladesh which says "no such answer which a witness shall be compelled to give, shall subject him to arrest or prosecution or be proved against him in any criminal proceeding except a prosecution for giving false evidence by such answer". The USA Supreme Court adopted a liberal interpretation and allowed constitutional right to silence in not only criminal cases but also in civil cases.[35] But this right to silence as enshrined in Article 35(4) of the Constitution of Bangladesh covers the criminal cases only. It mandates that an accused cannot be compelled to be a witness against himself.

On the contrary the provision of Section 132 of Evidence Act 1872 may appear to contravene the provision of Article 35(4), but in fact this Article remains unaffected by Section 132. Because Section 132 deals with the witness whereas Article 35(4) deals with the accused and as has previously been shown an accused and witness in a case may not be the same person.

The guarantee provided under Article 35(4) of the Constitution of Bangladesh is against the compulsion to be a witness that means making of oral or written statements in or out of the court by the accused. Such statements do not necessarily mean confessional statements, which have a reasonable tendency to point to the guilt of the accused. Bangladesh followed the liberal interpretation as to the extent of protection of the right to silence similar to the one given by the Supreme Court of India in the case of *Bombay vs. Kathi Kalu.*[36] In this case the court said that,

> "It is well established that Article 20(3) of the Constitution of India is directed against self incrimination by

> the accused person. Self incrimination must mean conveying information by the accused person based upon personal knowledge in giving information and cannot include merely the methodical process of producing document in the court which may throw a light on any of the points in controversy".

The Supreme Court of India previously did not apply the safeguard of witness against self-incrimination like the Supreme Court of USA i.e., the Supreme Court of India in interpreting Article 20(3) of the Constitution of India, which provides this right to a person who is accused of an offence, that is before claiming the privilege under the said Article there should be a formal accusation against the person claiming it. But in subsequent two cases[37] namely, *Narayanlal* and *Dastagir* case the court clarified the interpretation and extended the ambit of the rights to a person under Article 20(3). Even a person who was not an accused but was merely a suspect can also claim the right to silence. But in this respect Bangladesh has failed to give such a wide application of the right to silence.[38]

One of the main causes behind that is the society being ridden with corruption there remains an absolute chance of abuse. It is to be observed whether the Supreme Court of Bangladesh should be inclined to apply the protection in cases other than criminal prosecution.

RIGHT TO PROTECTION FROM UNLAWFUL SEARCH AND SEIZURE OF PROPERTY

Search is an inextricable step in the criminal justice, which is a drastic power of an invasion on the sanctity and privacy of citizen's home. Even though it is an encroachment upon some sort of fundamental rights still then people need to brook them for public interest. But at the same time it should be noted that the power of coercive search and seizure should not be abused by the authority under the camouflage of public interest. There should necessarily be some sort of balance between the search of individuals' property and public interest. So some safeguard must inevitably exist. In the context of criminal legislation of Bangladesh it strives to balance between these two interests. It may be brought in mind that the power to commit search in a place under the provision of Cr. P. C. is drastic, and undesirable use of it may frustrate the object for which it was incorporated under the provision of Section 96 of the Cr. P. C. It may cause loss of prestige and business of individuals. The criminal legislation of our country has tried to safeguard the individual against the arbitrary use of power by the authority. In Section 96 of the Cr. P. C. there are 3 grounds under which the police authority can search. Those grounds are (a) where the document or thing is known to be in possession of any person (b) where the court has reasons to believe that summons for production of anything will not be obeyed and (c) where a general search is considered necessary for the purpose of trial.

In the case of *H M Ershad vs. Bangladesh*[39] the question was raised before the court whether the search and seizure of property by authority in due course will not amount to violation of fundamental rights. Article 43 of the Constitution of Bangladesh provides that "every citizen shall have the right to be secured in his home against entry, search and seizure and to the privacy of the correspondence, and other means of communication." Thus, it is the constitutional requirement that no Police Officer or any public functionary shall be empowered to enter into the property of any citizen unless he is a person duly authorized by law.[40] It also provides that any such law, which so authorizes should be a law made in the interest of state security, public order and public morality. In the case of *Karak Sing vs. MP*[41] the Supreme Court of India said such a restriction should necessarily be reasonable restriction on the right, if the restriction imposed does not bear any nexus to the specified matter for which the restriction was imposed, or is excess of requirements for which it was made, or if the law does not provide a way of checking the arbitrary or illegal exercise of power than that order of search and seizure will not be valid.

In India domiciliary visit by police in a house of suspected person at night under the Police Regulation Act was held to be invalid in view of fundamental rights guaranteed by Article

21 in the Constitution of India. In Bangladesh such an act of search and seizure will encroach upon the fundamental rights guaranteed under Articles 31 and 32 of the Constitution of Bangladesh. The Constitution mandates such action by police as illegal. If a Police Officer enters into a place for the purpose of arresting somebody under Section 47 of Cr. P. C then that act of search by the Government will not be illegitimate. Because Section 47 unequivocally permits a person acting under the warrant of arrest to enter any premises to effect arrest if he has reasons to believe that persons sought to be arrested can be found in that premises. And Section 97 of the Cr. P. C. authorizes the court to issue such a search warrant under certain specified condition and should apply its mind to the facts and circumstances of the case.[42] But in Section 97 only home has been inserted but the word 'home' should be considered from a liberal point of view. In USA the word house has been given an extended meaning, which also includes the business premises within the protection of fourth amendment of the Constitution of USA.[43]

Article 43 of the Constitution of Bangladesh expressly relates to home and in view of the language it does not include business premises. In view of Article 31 the business property of any person cannot be subject to search and seizure without the jurisdiction of law. On the other hand the Constitution of USA works in a more comprehensive field in respect of search and seizure in the persons' houses, papers and effects also. Therefore in the *Silverman v. US*[44] the court says the fourth amendment recognises the right of a man to retreat into his own home and there be free from unreasonable governmental intrusions. Under the US jurisdiction a person's house cannot be searched by police without fulfilling some conditions i.e., there should be a search warrant issued by an impartial Magistrate, the Magistrate should be satisfied of some probable cause.

In a case of English jurisdiction Camder L. J. says every invasion of private property be it ever so minute is a trespass. No one can set foot upon my ground without my licence. But it is to be borne in mind that the fourth amendment of the Constitution of USA is not an absolute bar. It has some necessity and rationale behind to deter intentional illegality on the part of the police and the rule is extended where its benefit as a deterrent outweighs the social cost of its use. In this respect India and Britain took a suitable interpretation. In Bangladesh perspective it is considered that as non-application of exclusionary rule has the effect of undermining Article 31 of the Constitution cf Bangladesh, which would ensure to serve exploitation by police. So exclusionary rule is necessary here as the police can obtain a search warrant from the court.[45]

EVIDENTIARY VALUE OF ILLEGAL SEARCH AND SEIZURE

Now the question is whether the results of an illegal search and seizure can be used as evidence in trial or in inquiry. In answer to the above-mentioned question, the Supreme Court of USA held that the fourth amendment barred the introduction of evidence procured through unlawful search and seizure.[46] The rationale behind such was to bar the intentional illegality on part of police and the rule is extended where its benefit as a deterrent outweighs the social cost of its use.[47] In USA such an exclusionary power is confined to criminal trial only. The British court viewed differently and ruled if justice is to be done then any sort of evidence should not be left. In India in the case of *Malakani vs. Maharastra*[48] the Supreme Court of India did not deny to accept the exclusionary rule of accepting evidence of USA procured in violation of Article 21 of the Constitution of India. In the perspective of Bangladesh the present performance of police demands the application of the exclusionary rule and no legitimate governmental interest can suffer by the application of the rule as the police can always obtain a search warrant from the court.[49]

SEARCH AND SEIZURE OF WOMEN ACCUSED

Due to the difference of sex, women are needed to be searched in a special way and the process of searching of a woman is totally different from that of a man. There exists particular provisions' regarding the search of women accused. Search may be of two kinds, the place suspected to be the abode of the accused may be required to be searched in order to find out and ensure about whether the accused is actually there. In that situation, the person acting under a warrant of arrest, or any Police Officer having authority to arrest has reason to believe that the person to be arrested has entered into, or is within, any place, the person residing in, or being in charge of, such place, shall, on demand of such person acting as aforesaid or such Police Officers, allow him free ingress thereto, and afford all reasonable facilities for a search therein.[50] If the demand mentioned above is not fulfilled then the person acting under a warrant of arrest or the Police Officer is empowered to break open any outer or inner door or window of any house or place, whether that be of the person to be arrested or of any other person.[51] If that place where the accused is suspected to be ıesiding is an apartment in the accused's occupancy of a woman, not being the person to be arrested, who according to custom, does not appear in public, such person or Police Officer shall, before entering such apartment, give notice to such woman that she is at liberty to withdraw and shall afford her every reasonable facility for withdrawing, and may then break open the apartment and enter it.[52] After arrest is made, the arrested person, male or female, may be searched by the Police Officer arresting the accused or in case of private individual, the Police Officer to whom the private individual makes over the arrested person and the search should be made in a safe custody.[53] All articles other than necessary wearing apparels found upon him may be searched. The female arrestees are, in a bit, taken under special provision in this case. If it becomes necessary to cause a woman to be searched, the search shall be made by another woman, with strict regard to decency.[54] So, the safeguards as to search of an accused woman by the LEA reveals that while searching any arrested woman, the rules of decency that is the assurance of honesty, politeness in behaviour that follows the accepted moral standards and shows respect for others should be strictly followed to its entirety. Another meaning of this is that while searching an accused woman utmost respect and honour have to be shown to the magnanimity of her privacy. Inviolability of her privacy as a female should be given due respect.[55]

CONCLUSION

The organs of inquiry initiates criminal proceedings and are governed by the rules of criminal procedure, and carries out urgent acts of investigation to establish and record traces of crime: inspection, search, seizure, examination, detention and questioning of suspects and interrogation of injured persons and witnesses.[56] The organ of inquiry is obliged to inform the procurator of the discovery of crime and the opening of inquiry.

Criminal legislation of Bangladesh confers wide discretionary powers on the investigating authorities to make searches and seizure of property in the possession of the accused while conducting an investigation or an inquiry. At the same time they also contain specific provisions safeguarding the interests of the accused.[57] For that reason the administration of justice in each country insists that every person accused of an offence is interrogated and searched in accordance with the procedure established by law.

A person against whom criminal proceedings have been instituted has been conceded the right to keep silent about the accusation. This privilege has been conferred upon by the doctrine of presumption of the innocence, which is considered as a cardinal principle in the administration of criminal justice in all countries.

Since the safeguards accorded to the accused against unlawful search and seizure is likely to be in greater jeopardy at the interrogation and the investigation stages, it would be worth for making an appraisal of these safeguards as stipulated under the criminal legislation of Bangladesh.

NOTES

1. Salmond WG, *Jurisprudence,* (12th Edition; Maxwell: 1985), 88.
2. *Ibid.*
3. *See* Chapter 1.6.
4. Gibbons DC, *Society, Crime and Criminal Career,* (13th edition, Prentice Hall of India, Delhi: 1978), 56.
5. Kibria ABMG, *Police Administration in Bangladesh,* (First Edition, Jatya mudarn: 1976), 176.

6. *The Daily Prothom Alo,* Dhaka (Bangladesh), 18 May 2004. The website of the *Daily Prothom Alo* is: <*http://www.prothom-alo.net*>
7. Batra M, *Protection of Human Rights in Criminal Justice Administration,* (Deep & Deep Publications, New Delhi: 1989), 42.
8. Kelkar RV, *Outlines of Criminal Procedure,* (Deep & Deep Publications, New Delhi: 1984), 22.
9. Kibria ABMG, *supra note* 5 at 177-178.
10. Gross H, *Criminal Investigation,* (Fifth Edition, Sweet & Maxwell Ltd.: 1962)), 5.
11. II CWN 554.
12. *The Crown vs. Adalat,* 8 DLR (FC) 69.
13. 44 DLR 49.
14. *Ataur Rahman vs. The State,* 42 DLR (AD) 31.
15. 41 DLR 306.
16. *Abul Hossain vs. State,* 35 DLR 76.
17. *Golam A Maula vs. The State,* 46 DLR 140.
18. Batra M, *supra note* 7 at 44-46.
19. *Ibid.*
20. Kibria ABMG, *supra note* 5 at 177.
21. Batra M, *supra note* 7 at 45.
22. Phillips C., Cox G and Pease K, *World Factbook of Criminal Justice System: England and Wales,* p. 7.
23. Stephen JF, *A History of Criminal Law of England,* (London: 1883), 354; *see also* Lord Atkin's observation in *Lawrence vs. The King,* (1933), AC 699.
24. *Ajmer Sign vs. State of Punjab,* (1953), SCR 418.
25. *See,* Chapter 1.2.
26. *Nandini vs. Satiapathy,* SCC CN(1978) 236.
27. Batra M, *supra note* 7 at 48.
28. *Evidence Act 1872,* Section 139; this Section says, "A person summoned to produce a document does not become a witness by the mere fact that he produces it and cannot be cross examined unless he is called as a witness". *See also* Chapter 2.6.
29. *M.P. Sharma vs. Satish Chandra,* (1954) SCR 1077 at 1088.

30. Islam M, *Constitutional Law*, (BILIA, Dhaka, 4th Edition: 1995), 191.
31. Stephen J F, *A History of Criminal Law in England*, (London: 1883), 354.
32. David R and Khanna SL, *Comparative Law (History of Common Law)*, Oriental Publishers, 217.
33. *Counselman vs. Hitchcock*, 142 US 547.
34. Islam M, *supra note* 30 at 189.
35. *Malloy vs. Hagan*, 378 US 1; *Lefkownz vs. Cunningham*, 431 US 801.
36. AIR 1961 SC 1808.
37. AIR 1961 SC 29; AIR 1960 SC 756.
38. Islam M, *supra note* 30 at 190.
39. *H M Ershad vs. Bangladesh*, 52 DLR (AD) 162.
40. Islam M, *supra note* 30 *at* 241.
41. *Karak Sing vs. MP*, AIR 1963 SC 1295.
42. *Hoslide vs. Crown*, 44 CWN 82.
43. *Mashall vs. Barlours*, 98 SC 1816.
44. *Silverman v. US*, 365 US 505.
45. Islam M, *supra note* 30 at 241.
46. *Weeks vs. US*, 232 US 383; *Silrerthorne Lamber Co. vs. US*, 251 US 385.
47. *Frank vs. Delawse*, 98 SC (1978) 2674.
48. *Malakani vs. Maharastra*, AIR 1973 SC 157.
49. Islam M, *supra note* 30 at 243.
50. *Code of Criminal Procedure* 1898, Section 47.
51. *Code of Criminal Procedure* 1898, Section 48.
52. *Ibid.*
53. *Code of Criminal Procedure* 1898, Section 51
54. *Code of Criminal Procedure* 1898, Section 52
55. *Constitution of Bangladesh*, Article 43 and the *Universal Declaration of Human Rights* 1948, Article 12.
56. *CPC, RSFSR*, Article 119.
57. Batra M, *supra note* 7 at 136.

RIGHT TO A FAIR TRIAL AND THE PRISONERS RIGHTS 5

INTRODUCTION

The right to a fair trial[1] is a basic human right, which has been accorded to individuals by international human rights law as well as national law. This chapter seeks to correlate internationally and nationally protected human rights, which are applicable in the criminal process. The right to a fair trial and the jail situation in Bangladesh are set forth in detail and a comparison with the provisions of the UDHR and the ICCPR have been dealt with in this chapter. It will assist in evaluating whether criminal justice system of a country guarantees respect for international standards of fair trial.

The right to a fair trial has been accorded to individuals as human rights by international law, either by treaty or by customary law for over 50 years. This right is available from the moment when a person is arrested. This fundamental right is composed of both a general right and various sub-rights. All national and international instruments contain the notion of a fair trial, yet the term "fair trial" has not been defined precisely. It may contain the notion of equality before courts, designed to protect the individual from acts of authority which violate his/her basic human rights. In criminal proceedings the ICCPR grants basic fair trial rights for the individuals and state parties are obliged to provide this right to the accused within their jurisdiction.

This chapter is a guide to the international and national levels for the protection of the right to a fair trial. It is intended for the use of trial observers and others, assessing the fairness of an individual case.

RIGHT TO PUBLIC AND SPEEDY TRIAL

The right to a fair and public hearing before a tribunal in all suits at law and criminal matters pursuant to Article 14(1) of the ICCPR is the core of "due process of law".[2] All the remaining provisions in Articles 14(2) to 14(7) and Article 15 are specific formulations of the 'fair trial' in criminal cases. Article 14(1) contains an institutional guarantee that obligates the State Parties to take extensive, positive measures to ensure this guarantee. They must *set up* by law independent, impartial tribunals and provide them with the competence to hear and decide on criminal charges and on rights and obligations in suits at law. Such hearings must be fair and public and a criminal charge must conform with the other provisions of Articles 14 and 15. Finally all decisions in criminal matters must be pronounced publicly.[3]

Hearing before Courts

The guarantee of hearing by an independent and impartial tribunal established by law has been incorporated in Article 14 of the ICCPR. For fair hearing and fair trial independence of judges is a requirement, otherwise judges would not be able to make independent decision based on facts and cogent evidence without any commitment to any party or any public authority.[4]

For the impartiality it is required that a judge is not prejudiced with respect to the case before him, does not allow himself to be influenced by information from outside the court room, by rousing of public feelings, or by any pressure, but bases his opinion on objective arguments on the basis of what has been put forward during the trial and proceedings. The provision that the judicial tribunal must be 'established by law' implies the guarantee that the judicial organisation in a democratic society is not left to the discretion of the executive, but is regulated by law emanating from parliament.[5]

The Principle of Fair Hearing: 'Equality of Arms'

The ICCPR demands a fair hearing. Article 14(1) declares that all persons shall be equal before the courts and tribunals. The right of all persons to be equal before the courts requires that the prosecution and defence be treated equally in a criminal trial. The court cannot act in a way, which gives the prosecution an advantage over the defence.

Article 14(1) guarantees right to a *fair hearing* by a tribunal. This principle is at the centre of the criminal procedural guarantee and has been ensured by a number of ancillary rights in Articles 14 and 15 of the ICCPR. The right to a fair trial is broader than the 'minimum guarantees' of the accused provided by Article 14(3) of the ICCPR. Thus, although a criminal trial may fulfil all the requirements of Article 14(2) to (7) and Article 15, it may nevertheless conflict with the precept of fairness in Article 14(1).

The principle of a fair trial including *'equality of arms'* equally applies to *suits at law*. In *Morael vs. France*, a case concerning proceedings under the French Bankruptcy Law, the Committee interpreted the concept of a fair hearing "as requiring a number of conditions, such as equality of arms, respect for the principle of adversary proceedings, preclusion of *ex officio reformatio in pejus*, and expeditious procedure".[6] Whereas in *Munoz Hermoza vs. Peru*[7] the HRC held the French proceedings to be in conformity with these conditions, it found a violation of the justice be rendered without undue delay. This communication had been submitted by an ex-sergeant of the *Guardia Civil* (police) who had been dismissed from service for allegedly insulting a superior. The HRC held that administrative proceedings lasting for seven years constituted unreasonable delay and thus a violation of the right to a fair hearing under Article 14(1).[8]

Right to be Present at Trial

The accused has the right to appear in person before the court. Article 14(3)(d) of the ICCPR provides the accused with a right to be tried in his/her presence. He/she may give up this right if it is done voluntarily and in writing, and measures must be taken to ensure that counsel provides effective representation in the interests of justice.[9] But where the accused person is personally informed of the date, time and place of the trial and fails to appear for trial without any reasonable excuse, he/she may be tried in his/her absence. However, if the accused subsequently appears and shows that either inadequate notice was given, or some other good and valid reason prevented him/her from appearing, then he/she may be entitled to a new hearing.

A Uruguayan Professor, Hiber Conteris, charged with subverting the Constitution, criminal and political association, illegal entry, and kidnapping, was denied any opportunity to appear in person before a judge. He was convicted by a military tribunal *in absentia*. On appeal, he was not brought before members of the military tribunal who were reviewing his case, instead a junior officer confined himself to read out the sentence against him and asked for his signature".[10] The HRC found that both trial and appeal denied his right to a public trial in violation of Article 14 (1) of the Covenant.

Another Uruguayan tried by a military court challenged the fairness of a military procedure which permitted the accused to submit only written statements taken by a court clerk and did not allow her to be brought before the judge in person. The HRC requested that the state provide information on whether it allowed the accused to appear in person. When it received the state's routine assurance, the facts were placed in dispute. The Committee would not decide on an issue when the facts were disputed.[11] The precept of a fair hearing entails that the accused is entitled to be in person at his/her trial.[12] This view finds some support in the case law.[13] A number of complaints by or on behalf of the accused about trial out of their presence, which were directed against Uruguay, were found well founded by the HRC.[14]

Right to a Public Trial

Article 14 (1) of the ICCPR provides that the public may be excluded from a trial only for reasons of moral, public order, or national security in a democratic society, or where required by the private lives of the parties. Where a party is entitled to a public trial, the court must provide information about time and venue of the proceedings available to the public and must provide adequate facilities for the attendance of interested members of the public.[15] The public nature of trials obliges both the investigation agencies and the Prosecutor's Office strictly to observe legality in their activity preceding trial for whatever evidence they collect shall be subjected to testing in open session. The same responsibility is bestowed upon the witnesses, victims, experts, interpreters and persons involved in a case.

The principle of openness of court proceedings is undoubtedly an essential component of the right to defence of the accused. It acts as a check against judicial caprice or vagaries and serves as a powerful instrument for creating confidence of the public in fairness, objectivity and impartiality of the administration of justice. In Bangladesh the Cr. P. C. has not yet included this principle, but conventionally open hearing is provided in administering justice, which is a fundamental right under Article 35(3) of the Constitution of Bangladesh.[16]

Right to have Judgement made Public

Article 14(1) of the ICCPR provides that any judgement rendered in a criminal case or in a suit at law shall be made public except in juvenile proceedings or matrimonial disputes related to the guardianship of children for social security in the sense that if disputes regarding the above two matters are held in public that may impact negatively both on the society and the juvenile offender. Article 14(1) of the Covenant requires for criminal proceedings, that the hearing and the pronouncement of the judgement shall be public. Written judgement is one of the requirements of a fair trial.

In that context it will of course have to take into consideration the protection of the private life of the accused, as one of the expressly mentioned grounds of restriction, and the risk that may be involved in publicity for the presumption of innocence protected in the second paragraph of Article 14 of the ICCPR. The requirement of publicity applies in principle to all the successive phases of the proceedings.[17]

Right to Speedy Trial

The trial must take place 'within a reasonable time' is prescribed by Article 14 of the Covenant and the persons subject to criminal prosecution are entitled to a hearing 'without undue delay'. Article 9(4) of the ICCPR provides that anyone deprived of his/her liberty by arrest or detention is entitled to have a court decision without undue delay on the lawfulness of the detention.

Article 14 (3)(c) of the ICCPR guarantees an individual charged with a criminal offence the right to a trial without undue delay. The cases under this provision indicate that the right to trial without undue delay must be understood as the right to a trial, which produces a final judgement and sentence without undue delay.[18] The HRC found that in the absence of information about the outcome of the criminal proceedings or copies of the court decisions it cannot be said that an individual had been tried without undue delay and for that it is a violation of Article 14 (3)(c).[19]

Article 9(4) of the Covenant provides especially for persons detained on remand that they are entitled to trial within a reasonable time or to release. There the beginning of the period to be considered is evident: the moment of the arrest.[20]

An important component of a fair trial is the expeditious conduct of trial proceedings. The Constitutional protection accorded to the accused against an unlawful deprivation of his liberty would be meaningless if unnecessary delay is caused in his/her trial. Though the right to speedy trial has been specifically enumerated in Article 35(3) as a fundamental right in the Constitution of Bangladesh the right can be implicitly inferred from other Articles of the Constitution.[21] In this context the Supreme Court of India has interpreted Article 21 of the Indian Constitution in *Hussainara Khatoon vs. State of Bihar,*[22] as conferring a right to speedy trial, which was reaffirmed in *State of Maharashtra vs. Champalal.*[23]

In *Hussainara Khatoon's* case, the Supreme Court of India held that since a "reasonably expeditious trial is an integral part of the fundamental right to life and liberty enshrined in Article 21" any accused who has been denied this right can, as of right invoke it. The court also held that the state is under a constitutional mandate to take all the necessary measures for securing this right to the accused. In its anxiety to protect and enforce the right to speedy trial the Supreme Court emphatically stated that no state should be permitted to deny this constitutional right.

By issuing such directions to the state the Supreme Court seems to have come closer to the realisation of the norms enshrined in clause (3) of Article 14 of the Covenant which lays down that any one who is charged with a criminal offence shall 'be tried without undue delay' and in Article 16 of the Draft Principles on Equality in the administration of justice which requires that everyone shall be guaranteed the right to a prompt and speedy trial.[24]

'Justice delayed is justice denied' is a well-known maxim and viewed from the angle of the accused person it recognises the right of the accused to a speedy trial so that there may be an early end to the proceedings against him/her resulting in acquittal or conviction. Thus, in the presence of a right to speedy trial in the Constitution of Bangladesh it is all the more pertinent for the criminal justice administration to strictly conform with expeditious disposal of cases.[25] In 2002 there was enacted a Speedy Trial Tribunal Act[26] in Bangladesh for quick disposal of certain cases transferred by the Government to the Tribunal by Gazette notification.[27]

GUARANTEES OF THE ACCUSED IN CRIMINAL TRIALS

Presumption of Innocence

This right is often embodied under a general right of access to the courts and tribunals. It is the focal point of any concept of due process and all the other sub-rights are built on the premise contained in it. That premise applies to both the judgement and treatment accorded to the accused once he/she is placed in legal custody. It appears then as the guiding force in the formulation of the legal procedures or minimum standard of justice associated with right to a fair trial. The right to a legal defence, the right to counsel, to a transcript, etc., all stem from this basic premise that the accused is innocent until his/her guilt can be ascertained in a court of law.

Article 14(2) of the Covenant prescribes that everyone charged with a criminal offence must be presumed innocent until proved guilty according to law. This provision concerns a special aspect of the general concept of a fair trial in criminal cases. The most important aspect of the presumption of innocence concerns the foundation on which a conviction is based.[28] This aspect is very closely connected with the requirement of the court's impartiality. The court has to presume, without any prejudice, the innocence of the accused and may convict him only on the basis of evidence put forward during the trial,[29] which moreover has to pertain to the evidence recognised as such by the applicable law. These evidences have been presented by the prosecution and not by the court itself, while the accused must be given full opportunity to disprove these evidences.[30]

Right to Adequate Information on the Accusation

The right to adequate information is fundamental to the concept of a fair trial. Without it, an arbitrary arrest could not be questioned. It embodies not only the formal charges lodged against an accused, but extends to notification of the reasons for the arrest. In the fair trial context, such right may also include prior written notification of the reasons for the arrest,[31] as well as information about the time of arrest and the arresting authority,[32] which must be recorded and made available to the accused and his/her counsel.[33] It is necessary to allow the defence adequate preparation to defend against these charges.[34]

Right to an Appeal

Everyone has the right to appeal. Article 14(5) of the ICCPR provides that everyone convicted of a crime shall have the right to his/her conviction and sentence being reviewed by a higher tribunal according to law'. The right to an appeal may be considered part of the due process right and an extension of the right to a fair trial. It is also an important right of its own. It is found in only ICCPR and American Convention of Human Rights (ACHR), as a basis of the concept of justice. It consists of the right to have a judgement or conviction reviewed by a higher court or authority and the right to have the corresponding sentence or punishment examined as minimum guarantees found in the other rights.

In *Montejo vs. Colombia* the HRC held that a charge, which involved a one-year sentence, is enough to come within the purview of Article 14(5) and requires review by a higher tribunal regardless of whether domestic law viewed it as a "criminal charge".[35] It includes therefore the right to counsel, the right to an interpreter, their appointment if justice so requires, and because a transcript is also necessary in this context, it provides not only access to this document, but a free copy as well, in order that the appellant may prepare the appeal.

Right to Remedies and Compensation

Article 14(6) of the ICCPR provides that a person is entitled to compensation for punishment after a conviction, which is revered or pardoned on the basis of new or newly discovered facts, which conclusively show there has been a miscarriage of justice. Article 2 (3) (a) provides that any person whose rights under the Covenant have been violated shall have the right to seek an effective remedy.

RIGHT TO RELEASE PENDING TRIAL

Article 9(3) of the Covenant provides those detained or arrested on a criminal charge have the right to trial within a reasonable time or release. Detention of a person in custody must not only be lawful but reasonable and necessary in the circumstances.[36] The HRC examined the court-ordered detention of a lawyer who refused to co-operate in an investigation of his clients on the basis of lawyer-client privilege. The Netherlands argued that his nine-week detention was lawful and therefore did not violate Article 9. The Committee found that detention "must be interpreted more broadly to include elements of inappropriateness, in justice and lack of predictability".[37] The lawyer was being held in custody to ensure his accessibility for authorities carrying out a criminal investigation. The Committee found that the lawyer was not obliged to provide such co-operation; hence, the detention was neither necessary nor reasonable and violated Article 9(4).

The HRC held that suspicion of murder alone did not demonstrate a sufficient interest to justify pre-trial detention. An individual arrested in Ecuador for murder was detained for five years before indictment.[38] The Committee recognised that Article 9(3) allows legal authorities to hold a person in custody if it is necessary to assure that the accused appears at trial. The Ecuadorian authorities expressed no concern about the explanation for detaining the suspect without bail, the Committee found that the suspect must be granted a prompt trial or released. An incomplete criminal investigation does not justify keeping an individual in detention. Ecuadorian authorities argued that the detention was not prolonged[39] because the pre-trial investigation was completed just prior to indictment.[40] The HRC held that the entire trial must be complete to satisfy the prompt trial requirement. A complete trial involves a final judgement and the detainee is entitled to be released.

SENTENCING: CONVICTION OR ACQUITTAL

Right to Life and Liberty

The supreme human right is undoubtedly the right to life, and all other rights are subordinate to it. This right is enunciated in the UDHR and in the ICCPR. Article 3 of the UDHR states that "Everyone has the right to life". The ICCPR has stated vividly the right to life,[41] "Every human being has the inherent right to life". This right shall be protected by law that, "No one shall be arbitrarily deprived of his/her life". The death penalty can only be carried out pursuant to a final judgement rendered by a competent court.

Anyone sentenced to death shall have the right to seek pardon or commutation of the sentence. Amnesty, pardon or commutation of the sentence of death may be granted in all cases. Sentence of death shall not be imposed for crimes committed by persons below eighteen years of age and shall not be carried out on pregnant women.

Under the provisions of both UDHR and ICCPR the right to life is non-derogable and therefore, cannot be suspended under any circumstances. The right to life should not be too narrowly interpreted. The state is required to take all possible measures to reduce, infant child and adult mortality for increasing life expectancy. In this regard, urgent steps should to be taken to eliminate malnutrition and epidemics. Poor prison conditions that affect the health of prisoners may also fall within this provision.[42]

This right should take effect from the moment of birth and is broad enough to embrace the most specific principles as well as the most abstract and general ones. This right may specifically guarantee the freedom to conduct one's existence without fear of governmental threat or interference. In the abstract, however, it may guarantee to each individual a psychological sense of self or the freedom to grow, the freedom to make choices and have some control over the choices.

Under the ICCPR, States are not obliged to abolish the death penalty but to limit its use and in particular, to abolish it for other than the most serious crimes. The HRC has stated that by definition every execution of a sentence of death may be considered to constitute cruel and inhuman treatment within the meaning of Article 7. While the Article permits imposition of the death penalty, the wording suggests that abolition is desirable. The HRC considers abolition by countries to progress in the enjoyment of the right to life.

Discussion on the International Bill of Human Rights and the Constitution of Bangladesh reveals that the right to life is the top most right which must be protected irrespective of sex, race, language, colour, political opinion, birth or origin, and religious affiliation. In spite of all these documents in favour of right to life, it is found in Bangladesh that people of different sex, political activist, civilians, labour, maid-servants and even children are subjected to murder indiscriminately. Killing in Bangladesh has become an ordinary and daily affair. There is perhaps, not a single day when one or more persons are not killed. The pages of daily newspapers, journal of human rights and information from US State Department bear the testimony to the above statement. The strangest thing is that the right to life has been, besides others, infringed by the members of the LEA like Police, BDR and ANSAR. According to the report of a daily newspaper a housewife, the victim to gang rape was eventually killed by her husband who poured *kerosene oil* on her body and thereafter set fire. Her husband could not accept the fact of living with his raped wife.[43] His reaction was similar to honour killing in many Muslim countries.

Right to Freedom from Torture and Cruel, Unusual and Degrading Treatment or Punishment

It is the right to be free from torture, cruel, inhuman, or degrading treatment or punishment. In spite of constitutional guarantees of the right to be free from torture, inhuman, cruel and degrading punishment, both physical and psychological torture by the police like beating with a stick or rifle butt, electric shocks, pouring hot water in the nose, use of bar fetters etc., are widely reported in Bangladesh. Persons responsible for such crime are hardly convicted which encourage them to commit such inhuman activities again and again. In all international, regional and constitutional documents, this right of a person has been preserved carefully but not implemented properly.

Article 5 of the UDHR states, "No one shall be subjected to torture or to cruel, inhuman or degrading treatment or punishment". In the same language, the ICCPR also supports the preservation of this right against any kind of torture or punishment.[44]

Convention against Torture and other Cruel Inhuman or Degrading Treatment or Punishment, which was adopted by the General Assembly of the UN in 1984 and was enforced in 1987, states that no person shall be subjected to torture or to cruel, inhuman, or degrading punishment or treatment. Besides, we may quote the constitutional provisions of Pakistan regarding torture and inhuman punishment, "No person shall be subjected to torture for the purpose of extracting evidence".[45] The Constitution of Bangladesh also states "No person shall be subjected to torture or to cruel, inhuman or degrading punishment or treatment".[46] Article 29 of the Police Act 1861, which is in force in Bangladesh and Dhaka Metropolitan Police Ordinance 1976 also speak against torture. In spite of constitutional provision, torture, especially by the police and jail authority, has become a routine activity. Every day newspaper and human rights journals reported such sad incidents of torture, degrading punishment and inhuman treatment. A separate list has been supplied regarding torture and inhuman treatment by the members of LEA in Chapter 3. During 1996 in different newspapers and human rights journals about 226 rape cases on girls and women had been reported.[47]

Police arrested Sheema Chowdhury, a girl of 17 years and a garment factory worker in Chowkbazer under Chittagong District, on 8 October 1996 in the evening when she was walking with her fiancée. She was taken to Raojan thana where four policemen raped her at mid-night when the Officer in-charge (OC) left the police station. Sheema Chowdhury became unconscious as a result of rape.[48] After medical examination, the doctor gave report of gang rape. Consequently she died in the hospital and she was burnt into ashes according to the rituals of Hindu religion, though she embraced Islam. The newspapers and human rights journals daily reported many more similar inhuman cases of police brutality.

In 1997, 26 persons died in police and jail custody, out of whom 23 died in jail or under treatment of jail authorities and three in police custody, three persons lost their lives by police torture. Besides 28 persons were killed and 174 were injured by Police, BDR and ANSAR firing. Eleven women were raped by the members of the LEA. The actual figure is more than this because the unmarried girls and housewives do not report the incidents of rape for the fear of losing their prestige in the society.[49]

The incidents regarding police torture and consequential death are also reported in the *State of Human Rights 1997*.[50] The report shows the police brutality though there is no constitutional or any legal provision to allow torture by police.

WOMEN ACCUSED AT FAIR TRIAL

Right to a fair trial is one the fundamental human rights of every individual. Every individual should enjoy the facility to get justice regardless of the difference of sex, race, caste, colour, place of birth and so on and so forth. The Constitution of Bangladesh says that all are equal before law and are entitled to equal protection of law.[51] Every human being should be treated responding to all of the principles of natural justice. The women accused shall be provided with the right to consult with a lawyer of her own choice and no one shall be deprived of that for the sake of fair trial.[52] Each should be treated on the basis of the law in force at the time of the commission of offence.[53] None of the accused in police custody shall be prosecuted and punished for the same offence more than once.[54] Speedy and public trial by an independent or impartial court or tribunal established by law is a basic human right and none should be denied of that.[55] The accused under trial shall be guaranteed the right of not to be a witness against herself.[56] The accused if convicted shall not be subjected to torture or to cruel, inhuman, or degrading treatment or punishment.[57]

PRISON CONDITION

Confinement in prison symbolizes a system of punishment and also a sort of institutional placement of under-trials and suspects during the period of trial.[58] Since there cannot be a society without crime and criminals the institutions of prison is indispensable for every country.

The history of prisons in India and elsewhere clearly reflect the changes in society's reaction to crime from time to time. The system of imprisonment represents a curious combination of different objectives of punishment. Thus prison may serve to deter the offender or it may be used as a method of retribution or vengeance by making the life of the offender miserable and difficult. The isolated life in prison and incapacity of inmates to repeat crime while in the prison fulfils the preventive purpose of punishment. It also helps in keeping crime under control by elimination of criminals from the society. That apart, prison may also serve as an institution for the reformation and rehabilitation of offenders. It therefore, follows that whatever be the object of punishment, the prison serves to keep offenders under custody and control.[59]

The modern prison system of Bangladesh is essentially based on the British Prison model, which in itself is an outcome of prison developments in America during the late eighteenth century. The following Acts and Regulations regulate the establishment and management of jails, the confinements and treatments of person therein, and maintenance or discipline amongst them:

The Prisons Act, No. IX of 1894, as amended

The Prisoners Act, No. V of 1871, as amended

The Prisoners Act, No. V of 1900, as amended

Regulation No III of 1818 *(Bengal Code) for the confinement of State Prisoners*

Those provisions of the *Code of Civil Procedure* (Act V of 1908), the *Code of Criminal Procedure* (Act V of 1898 as amended), and the *Penal Code* (Act XLV of 1860), which relate to the confinement of prisoners, the execution of sentences, appeals, lunatics and the like, must also be complied with in connection with prison administration.[60]

The Prisons Act, 1894 popularly known as Jail Code was legislated by the British rulers with provisions for severe punitive treatment with prisoners and primarily to serve their political purpose. In this Act, Prison is defined as "any jail or place used permanently or temporarily under the general or special orders of the Government for detention of prisoners and includes all lands, buildings, apartments thereto".[61]

Inhumane Prison Condition

Article 7 of the ICCPR prohibits torture and cruel, inhuman, or degrading treatment or punishment, and applies to the pre-trial period as well as other periods of detention. Article 10 provides that all persons deprived of their liberty shall be treated with humanity and respect.

No prisoner can be subjected to compulsory experiment while in detention or prison. A Uruguayan journalist was sentenced to seven years imprisonment for subversive association with an opposition political party. While in prison, the journalist was subjected to psychiatric experiments. For three years he had been injected, against his will, with tranquillisers every two weeks. When he refused, he was forcibly subdued, injected with the drug, and subsequently held incommunicado in a punishment cell for 45 days. The Committee found that this was an inhuman treatment and violated Articles 7 and 10 (1).[62]

Human Rights Fact-finder in 1997 published a news that two persons died in jail custody , one stated that punishments he (was) received in jail custody have already mentioned in Chapter 2.7.[63]

Fettering in iron chains and handcuffs is one of the common ways of torture in Bangladesh. Regarding this the *Prisons Act* 1894 provides that whenever the Superintendent considers it necessary for the safe custody of prisoners that they should be confined in irons, he may be subjected to secure rules and instructions as may be laid down by the Inspector General with the sanction of the Government, to confine them.[64]

To fetter prisoners in irons is an inhumanity unjustified save where safe custody is otherwise impossible. Although the routine resort to handcuffs and irons bespeaks of a barbarity hostile to human dignity and social justice yet this unconstitutionality is heartlessly popular in many penitentiaries so much so a penitent law must prescribe its use in any but the gravest situation.[65]

There are sufficient guidelines in Section 56, which contain a number of safeguards against misuses of bar fetters by the Superintendent. Section 56 does not permit the use of bar fetters for an unusually long period, day and night, and that too when the prisoner is confined in secure cells from where escape is somewhat inconceivable. Therefore, Section 56 of the Act is not violative of the Constitution.[66] Only the misuse of this Section, we can say, is violative of the human rights as well as the Constitution.

Prohibited Treatment

Prolonged judicial proceedings could constitute cruel, inhuman, or degrading treatment or punishment. A warrant of execution causes intense anguish to the individual concerned and a delay in proceedings regarding the warrant may constitute cruel, inhuman, or degrading treatment. Two men under a death warrant were granted a stay of execution 45 minutes before the scheduled time of execution. Authorities kept them in their death cell for twenty hours after the stay was granted. The Committee held that the delay in removing the men constituted cruel and inhuman treatment within the meaning of Article 7.[67]

A detainee's rights under Article 10 of the ICCPR include the right to adequate medical care during the detention and extend to persons under a sentence of death. The HRC considered allegations of a prisoner on death row that he was detained with denial of necessary ophthalmologic and dental treatment. The HRC found insufficient facts to decide the issue but affirmed that a person imprisoned under a death sentence cannot be detained without medical treatment.[68]

Incommunicado Detention Prohibited

Holding an individual incommunicado for a substantial period is a form of ill treatment and violates Article 10 of the ICCPR. The Committee examined the case of a Uruguayan student detained 14 months for subversive association.[69]

Article 14(3)(6) of the ICCPR provides that the accused should be given adequate time and facilities for the preparation of his defence and to communicate with counsel of his own choosing. Violations of the right to communicate with counsel have been found in a number of cases. For example, in *Wight vs. Madagascar*,[70] there was a breach "because during a 10 month period ... when criminal charges against him were being investigated and determined....[the victim] was kept incommunicado without access to legal counsel." The Committee has also commented upon Article 14(3)(b) of the ICCPR as follows:

> What is 'adequate time' depends on the circumstances of each case, but the facilities must include access to documents and other evidence, which the accused requires to prepare his case. Furthermore, Article 14(3)(b) requires the counsel to communicate with the accused in conditions giving full respect for the confidentiality of their communications. Lawyers should be able to counsel and to represent their clients in accordance with their established professional standards and judgment without any restrictions, influences, pressures or undue interference from any quarter.[71]

The right of the accused to communicate with counsel of his own choosing was inserted in the 3rd Committee of the General Assembly upon motion by Israel.[72] An analogous provision can be found in Article 8(2)(d) of the ACHR, but not in Article 6 of the ECHR. Typical violations of this right stem from cases of *incommunicado* detention[73] or when an ex-officio defence attorney has been appointed for the accused against his will.[74] Impermissible interference with the right to preparation of defence was found in a large number of other cases against Uruguay, Panama, Zaire, Jamaica and Madagascar.[75]

Standard Minimum Rules for the Treatment of Prisoners

Under trial prisoners are presumed to be innocent and shall be treated as such. Article 14(2) of the ICCPR enunciates, "Everyone charged with a criminal offence shall have the right to be presumed innocent until proved guilty according to law." Without prejudice to legal rules for the protection of individual liberty or prescribing the procedure to be observed in respect of untried prisoners, these prisoners shall get benefit by a special regime.

HUMAN RIGHTS AND JAIL SITUATION IN BANGLADESH

In the age of British rulers the Prisons Act were provided for severe punitive treatment with the prisoners and to serve primarily their political purpose. In those days important political leaders were detained in order to stop political movement against British rule. Around one hundred and eleven years passed (approximately) after the legislation of the Jail Code in 1894, but no effective measures have been taken to convert the penal institution into a reformatory one. Like the British rule, in Bangladesh political opposition leaders are kept inside the jail and are tortured by the jail authority. Several detainees have given their written statements regarding inhuman torture in the jail. Though two separate jail commissions were formed, one in 1957 and another in 1980, but the recommendations of the commission were not implemented in full to improve the fate of the prisoners.

Types of Prisons and Capacity thereof

In Bangladesh there are four types of jails (i) Central Jails, (ii) District Jails (iii) Subsidiary Jails and (iv) Thana Jails. These classifications are made as per Section 60(a) of the Prisons Act, 1894. There are 80 Jails in total in Bangladesh.[76]

Central Jails

There are nine Central Jails in Bangladesh located at Dhaka, Rajshahi, Jessore, Comilla, Chittagong, Sylhet, Rangpur, Barisal and Mymensingh. In these jails under trial prisoners, convicted prisoners sentenced to different terms including death and life imprisonment and also detainees are confined. In these jails maximum-security measures are taken.

District Jails

There are 55 District Jails, which are located in the District Head Quarters. In these jails all types of prisoners are confined except prisoners of over 5 years imprisonment.

Subsidiary Jails

All the subsidiary jails have been converted into District Jails.

Thana Jails

There are 16 Police Station Jails. These are located at thana head quarters.

The total registered capacity of these jails is 24000. According to one report in 1997 the number of prisoners were 44285.[77] But another report says that actual number is more and that is three to four times of the actual capacity. According to Maanobadhikar, 31August 1999, the total number is 93000. All jails are over-crowded and completely unsuitable to live. Prisoners are often deprived of the rights provided in the Jail Code. The statistics stated here shows the nature of over-crowdedness.[78]

Overcrowding and unhygienic conditions have made prisons unfit for human habitation. On reason for the lack of attention in the prisoners, particularly convicts, are perceived by the administration and the public as not deserving of humane treatment. Prisons are seen as penitentiary institutions and not for rehabilitation of the prisoners.

BRCT generally collects information on jail inmates through its fact-finding team as well as from the daily newspapers and magazines. A report was published in *The Weekly Robber*[79] that actual capacity of jails in Bangladesh is about 23,600 inmates whereas the jails are crowded with 34,507 inmates.[80] After one year, in 2000, *The Weekly Robber* published a report that the capacity of jails in Bangladesh is 23942 whereas 59885 jail inmates were staying in miserable condition in different jails of Bangladesh.[81] According to a newspaper[82] in 2001 prisons hold three times more prisoners than the total capacity.

This disproportionate increase in number created a severe space constrains and prisoners are forced to sleep by rotation. This situation may have contributed to a high prevalence of skin diseases and other ailments. The reasons for such over crowding are mainly long delays in trials, non-release of foreign prisoners and negligence of the prison administration.

The capacity of prisons and the number of prisoners throughout Bangladesh are as follows:[83]

Year	*Capacity*	*Actual number of Prisoners*
2001	24997	66625
2000	23942	59885
1999	23942	52370
1998	22439	47764
1997	21620	45174
1996	21620	44720
1995	21257	42992
1994	21247	41703

Source: *Good Prison Management,* BLAST and PRI and Odhikar (January-October 2001).

The authority has tried to increase the capacity of prisons over the years. The numbers of prisoners have also increased specially leaving the prison in a worse condition.

A study of some jails also casts a gloomy picture about jail situation in 1995, which discloses the deteriorating human rights situation of the prisoners about over-crowdedness.[84]

Sl. No.	*Name of Jail*	*Registered capacity*	*Total number of prisoners*	*More than capacity in percentage (%)*
1.	Bagerhat District Jail	130	744	610%
2.	Brahman Baria District Jail	191	549	257%
3.	Chuadanga District Jail	99	402	406%
4.	Cox's Bazar District Jail	140	910	650%
5.	Gazipur District Jail	70	325	464%
6.	Gaibandha District Jail	114	230	201%
7.	Kishorgonj District Jail	201	1035	514%
8.	Mowlovi Bazar District Jail	154	257	166%
9.	Narail District Jail	32	250	781%
10.	Nilphamari District Jail	94	205	218%
11.	Bogra District Jail	433	1380	318%
12.	Magura District Jail	46	311	676%
13.	Meherpur District Jail	38	100	263%
14.	Nowgaon District Jail	101	569	563%
15.	Pabna District Jail	521	937	179%
16	Noakhali District Jail	348	1800	517%
17.	Satkhira District Jail	80	859	1073%

Contd...

Sl. No.	Name of Jail	Registered capacity	Total number of prisoners	More than capacity in percentage (%)
18.	Sirajganj District Jail	165	442	267%
19.	Sunamganj District Jail	104	550	528%
20.	Narayanganj District Jail	126	775	615%
21.	Potuakhali District Jail	286	375	131%
22.	Jamalpur District Jail	177	500	282%
23.	Dhaka Central Jail	2300	8000	347%
24.	Chittagong Central Jail	747	4000	535%
25.	Comilla Central Jail			
26.	Rajshahi Central Jail	1277	3187	250%

According to newspapers prisoners are extremely overcrowded. The capacity and the actual presence of prisoners in 1998 could be seen as follows:[85]

Areas	Prison Capacity	Presence of prisoners
Dhaka Central Jail	2300	7500
Bogra District Jail	433	1380
Cox's Bazar District Jail	74	750
Chuadanga District Jail	39	240
Gazipur District Jail	70	325
Gaibandha District Jail	114	230
Jamalpur District Jail	117	500
Kishoreganj District Jail	201	1033
Magura District Jail	46	311
Meherpur District Jail	38	100
Moulavibazar District Jail	154	257
Narail District Jail	34	250
Naogaon District Jail	101	569
Narayanganj District Jail	126	775
Nilphamari District Jail	94	205
Noakhali District Jail	348	1800
Pabna District Jail	521	937
Patuakhali District Jail	286	375
Rajbari District Jail	73	200
Satkhira District Jail	80	859
Sirajganj District Jail	165	452
Sunamganj District Jail	104	550
Total: 22	5518	19598

No action has been taken by the government to remedy the situation, although the civil society and the media have become critical regarding the overcrowding of prisons.

A remarkable information may be noted here that nowadays most of the inmates of these overcrowded jails are the pre-trail prisoners. A report revealed that the number of under trial prisoners detained in jails in the country has increased in the last five years while that of convicts has decreased during the same period. Under trial prisoners were numbered to 26,000 in 1995 and their number rose to 37500 in 1999 but the number of convicts fell to 13422 from 15730 over this period. There were 41730 prisoners under trial and convicts in the jail in 1995 while the number rose to 50922 in 1999. Capacity of the 64 jails[86] including nine central jails across the country increased to 23942 from 21257 during the period.[87]

During the 60s, convicts numbered more than under-trial prisoners but the situation turned reverse in the '70s. The ratio of convicts and under trial prisoners became 25:75 in the '70s. The situation improved in the '80s and the ratio became 40:60. This happened due to 'Speedy trial' in summary courts under martial law. In '90s, the ratio again started charging in the opposite direction. It is true that many convicts were released on general amnesty in 1991 but the lengthy process of trial kept many accused detained in the jails as under trial prisoners. Normally, two thirds of any jail is earmarked for convicts and one third for under trial prisoners.[88]

Human rights activist and lawyer Elina Khan said the number of under-trial prisoners is increasing but that of convicts is decreasing because of the 'lengthy process of our legal system.' Lack of proper investigation and delays in submission of charge sheet are also responsible for the present situation.[89]

The present number may be greater than the above statistics on account of abuse of the SPA, 1974.

Types of Prisoners

Prisoners are of two types–

(i) Criminal prisoners; and

(ii) Convicted prisoners

Criminal prisoners are those prisoners who are duly committed to jail either under writ or warrant or order of any court or authority exercising criminal jurisdiction or by order of court martial. They are accused or under trial prisoners. Convicted prisoners are those prisoners who are committed to jail under sentence of a court or court martial and include a person detained in prison under Chapter VIII of the Cr. P. C. or under the Prisons Act, 1894.

Classifying the prisoners' Chapter XV of the Jail Code says that in evening jail each of the following classes shall be kept entirely separate from others:[90]

1. Civil prisoners.
2. Under trial prisoners.
3. Female prisoners.
4. Male prisoners under twenty one years of age.
5. Male prisoners who have not arrived at the age of puberty.
6. Other male convicted prisoners.

This Code also provided that in every jail, separate hospitals shall be provided for male and female prisoners.[91] Actually this type of accommodation is not provided to female prisoners. In Comilla Central Jail, which was established in 1829, among 75 bed of the hospital only 2 beds are allotted for the female[92] since the number of female prisoners is few. This is a common phenomenon of every jail.

Management in the Jail

In order to improve the jail condition, the Prison Reform Committee (PRC) recommended some suggestions but the government failed to implement these recommendations either due to paucity of fund or due to lack of seriousness. The PRC recommended for quick disposal of cases, fundamental changes in the jail code to make it contemporaneous, appointment of a psychologist and social welfare officer, separate prison for life imprisonment of grievous offenders and allocating adequate funds to prison authorities to bear necessary expenses.[93]

The prisoners in different jails are leading an inhuman life. The common problems with the prisoners are innumerable. Inadequate space, unhealthy environment, insufficient food and water, improper sanitation, absence of medical facilities and oppression by so-called masters make the lives of the prisoners miserable. We receive this information of violations of human rights through newspapers and human rights journals almost everyday.

Some of the examples may be cited here to prove the above statement. In Chittagong jail 75 Tuberculosis (TB) patients were sent, while the capacity of this jail hospital is 40. No special initiative is taken by the authority for these prisoners. As a result this infectious disease spread to the other prisoners. In Rajshahi Central Jail, which was established in 1840, there are only 2 latrines for 115 female prisoners.[94]

Due to overcrowding of the prisons by the under trials, the living condition of the prison is really deplorable. This is nothing but the denial of the legal rights and human rights of the prisoners. Some times they sleep by turns due to limited space. This is very pathetic. Prisoners are supplied with small quantity of very poor quality food, mostly due to the corrupt practices of certain categories of prison officers and partly due to overcrowding.[95] The most pathetic situation in the jails is that the ordinary prisoners are to take their meals sitting on the ground under the sky at all seasons. This is the report given by a retired Deputy Inspector General (DIG) of prison.[96]

It is expected that life of a prisoner will be more secured in jail than outside, for a prisoner is confined within the four walls where no outsider is allowed to enter without the permission of the jail authorities. The real state of fact is that each year a number of prisoners die in the jail custody by the torture of jail police or otherwise. Reports received from different newspapers and human rights journals reveal the death casualty in different jails of Bangladesh.[97]

In 1998 according to a newspaper report, 52 people died in prison, which is mentioned above. Among these 52 people there was a baby of 45 days and 4 foreign citizens. Among these deaths 24 occurred under Dhaka Central Jail, 5 in

Year	*Number of deaths*	*Name of Jails*
1990	23	Not available
1991	17	Dhaka, Chitagong, Jessore, Khulna, Comilla, Narsingdi and Feni
1992	16	Jessore, Bogra, Dhaka, Feni, Rangpur, Joypurhat, Bagherhat and Pirozpur
1994	31	Dhaka, Sylhet, Chittagong, Jessore, Comilla, Rajshahi, Madaripur, Jhalkathi, Barisal, Hobiganj, Magura, Banderban, Potuakhali, Dinajpur and Narsingdi
1995	10	Dhaka, Pabna, Sylhet, Bogra, Kushtia, B. Bariya and Chuadanga
1996	29	Jessore, Dhaka, Rangpur, Madaripur, Nowgaon, Cox's Bazar, Sylhet, B. Bariya, Meherpur, Manikganj and Panchogar
1997	23	Dhaka, Jessore, Rajshahi, Narayanganj, Chittagong, Faridpur, Kishorganj, Hobiganj, Sirajganj, Borisal, Mymensingh, Chandpur, Jhalkathi, Narail and B. Bariya
1998	52	
1999	30	

Chittagong District Jail, 3 in Khulna District Jail, 3 in Comilla Central Jail, 3 in Jessore Central Jail, 1 in Rajshahi Central Jail, 2 in Khagrachari District Jail, 2 in Netrokona District jail, 2 in Sylhet District Jail and 1 each in Chuadanga, Feni, Gaibandha, Gazipur, Manikgonj, Noakhali and Thakurgaon District jail.[98]

In 1999 according to the newspapers report, 30 persons died in prison. Among these 30 deaths 2 occurred under Dhaka Central Jail, 1 in Bhola Jail, 1 in Faridpur jail due to burning by fire, 1 in Mymensingh Central Jail. Rest 8 died in different jails as reported by *Manobadhikar*, May 1999.

Torture in jail custody is hardly seen by the public, nevertheless the death rate in jail custody is not insignificant. During the reporting period of BRCT in 2000, 26 prisoners died in jail or police custody without the torture of LEA. Among the deaths 3 were at Thana custody and 53 were at jail custody. The causes of these deaths were diseases, victimized by mass beating before arrest, age etc. The highest number was in

Dhaka Central Jail i.e. 18 prisoners died here and second highest was in Chittagong Central Jail comprised of 7 prisoners.[99]

It can be said that death tolls to such a number mainly for lack of proper medical treatment. The Jail Code provides that the barracks and cells shall be unlocked at dawn throughout the year. After the barracks have been opened and the prisoners counted out, they shall be marched to the latrine and be made to sit in file at a short distance therefrom, whilst those who wish to do so are allowed to visit the latrine in turn. During this parade those prisoners who are sick shall be made to sit a little apart from the rest, and shall be inspected by the Medical Subordinate, who shall see that they get such treatment as is necessary, but if any prisoner appears to be seriously ill he shall be sent to the Medical Subordinate at once.[100] It also provided in Jail Code that one of the important duties of the Medical Officer is to keep under his immediate supervision those prisoners who are below the normal standard of health or whose physical condition or previous history appear to indicate a predisposition to disease.[101]

But those provisions are not followed by the jail authority in most of the cases. The prisoners with infectious disease are kept with the normal prisoners which proliferate the disease among the normal prisoners. Due to the lack of proper medical check up and treatment the prisoners face death. It may be assumed that the Jail Code does not have sufficient logistic support to provide due rights to the prisoners as it was enacted at British period just for suppressing the native Indian. The jail authority should make arrangements to give training to its staffs from time to time so that they learn to handle the prisoners humanly. This way the deteriorating condition of prison will gradually improve.

Another report of Ain O' Shalish Kendra (ASK) revealed that most of the deaths were reported to have been caused by sickness. It was frequently reported that genuine sick detainees are often not admitted in the jail hospital, because payment of a bribe enables another influential detainee, who may not have been sick, to enjoy the moderately better and less cramped accommodation in a jail hospital for several months. It may be concluded that the provisions pertaining to a sick prisoner under Sections 741 and 742 of the Jail Code are ignored.[102]

In order to get the actual state of human rights in the jail an interview was made with the following under trial prisoners who had been in the Rajshahi Central Jail for a long period.[103] Their bail petitions were rejected several times.[104]

Name of the prisoner	*Age*	*Duration in the Jail*	*Number of times the bail petition are refused*
Joyenuddin	30	14 months	8
Ruhul Amin	35	18 months	15
Atoar Rahman	40	12 months	20
Sohrab Hossain	32	27 months	20
Abul Kalam Azad	28	14 months	19
Abul Kalam Azad (1)	32	27 months	20
Golam Mortoza	28	2 months	3
Md. Alal Uddin	26	7 months	3
M. Tarab Ali	42	2 months	3
Md. Ashraful Alam	35	4 months	5
Md. Abdul Mannan	32	12 months	12
Md. Sayedur Rahman	26	5 months	6

All of the above prisoners complained that the standard of food is very low and space is very small. They also reported that their bail petitions were rejected by the courts several times and they lead a very inhuman life in the jails.

The victims of prison injustice, particularly those who were poor and helpless and could not afford legal representation, have not been protected against torture and harassment. A victim of custodial torture can move the court directly through writ petition for protection of his fundamental rights, specially the right to life and liberty guaranteed by the Constitution though it is very expensive.

In India the Supreme Court's judicial activism for protecting the rights of prison inmates and detainees is discerned from a series of cases decided by the court. In *Prabhakar Pandurag vs. State of Makarastra*[105] the apex court ruled that detention in prison couldn't deprive the detenu of his fundamental rights. Following the same rule, the Supreme Court in *DBM Patnaik vs. State of AP*[106] held that mere detention is no ground for suspension of detenu's fundamental rights. In the historic judgment of *Sunil Batra vs. Delhi Administration*[107] the Supreme Court held that prisoners are entitled to all fundamental rights, which are consistent with their incarceration. In *Hussainara Khatoon,*[108] the Supreme Court of India observed that a procedure which does not make legal service available to a poor under-trial person cannot be regarded as just, fair and reasonable and, therefore, violative of right to legal aid of the poor accused as contemplated by Article 21 of the Constitution of India. The court in this case ordered release of those under-trials who were languishing in jails for an inordinately long period. In *Sheela Barse vs. State of Maharastra*[109] the Supreme Court of India on a complaint of custodial violence to women prisoners in jails directed that those helpless victims of prison injustice should be provided legal assistance at the state cost and protected against torture and maltreatment. In *Sanjay Suri,*[110] the apex court held that the prison authorities should change their attitude towards prison inmates and protect their human rights for the sake of humanity.

Case law in Bangladesh in the context of under trial prisoners is nonexistent. In view of the violation of human rights in the jail of Bangladesh the following recommendations are suggested to ameliorate worsening condition of the prisoners.

(i) The number of jail is to be increased in order to accommodate the prisoners with sufficient space for them to live in.

(ii) Proper supervision by the respective Deputy Commissioners and District Judges of concerned districts should be done so that the prisoners can communicate their grievances and on the basis of complaints remedial measures may be taken.

(iii) Delay in quick disposal of the case is the most important cause of over-crowdedness in the jail. More courts are to be established with sufficient number of judges so that the under-trial prisoners and detainees may either be convicted or acquitted or released as the case may be. This will reduce the number of inmates of the prisons and the problem of over-crowdedness will be solved to a great extent.

(iv) Proper sanitation is to be maintained in order to improve the present unhygienic condition.

(v) The quality and quantity of food must be improved.

(vi) Medical treatment and medical care are to be ensured.

(vii) Reformative arrangement for the convicts and under-trial prisoners may be made to improve their moral character so that after their release they may lead a better life.

(viii) Provision may be made for the detainees so that they can file writ petition to their respective district courts instead of *writ* to High Court Division. This can be done by amending the Constitution.

(ix) Besides, punitive measures must be taken against those jail authorities who are responsible for the unnecessary sufferings of the prisoners. Bribe is to be stopped in iron hand. It has been reported in different human rights journals that the prisoners are forced to offer bribe, otherwise they are tortured in different techniques.

In recent years some penologist of India have advocated the need of spiritual training for those who are condemned and incarcerated in prison cells. They shortly believe that the practice of *yoga* and meditation will enable the prisoners to control the evils of *kama, krodha, mada* and *lobha* which dwell in human body and help in gaining control over these evil forces so as to turn him a good man and a good citizen. This is indeed a new approach to penological problem of crime and criminals in the Indian setting. As rightly observed by Mr. Justice Ram Pal Singh of the High Court of Delhi, "human body is a temple where the deity of *atma* and *parmatma* reside. For keeping the temple of flesh and blood, the abode of good and bad, the sages and saints have prescribed *shadhna* by regular practice of *yoga, which* shall keep the human body not only healthy and strong but also neat, clean and pure. Healthy people would avoid crime and try to do good to the society by establishing peace and tranquillity".[111] Thus by the practice of yoga in prisons crimes can be considerably controlled and hardened criminals can be reformed. Undauntedly, the idea is laudable and must be adopted in practice. Inspired by this idea, many state governments of India have made training in yoga compulsory for prison inmates along with religious discourses.[112] Bangladesh can borrow this idea to reform the prisoners with such practices as are suitable to its society and culture.

RIGHT OF WOMEN PRISONERS IN BANGLADESH

The life of the prisoners both male and female in Bangladesh is regulated by the provisions set out in the Jail Code of Bangladesh. The male and female prisoners are generally classified into under-trial prisoners and convicted prisoners. Besides, there also exist provisions for the children and juvenile prisoners. Life of each class of the prisoners is regulated by some general and special type of provisions contained in the Jail Code. The Jail Code provides that the female prisoners shall be kept in a ward totally separated from the male prisoners and even the under-trial female prisoners, if possible shall be kept apart from the convicts. There shall be a separate hospital for the female prisoners. Everything shall be conducted by the Jailor in the female enclosure. In this regard, the provisions of the Jail Code run as follows:

> Female prisoners shall be rigidly secluded from the male prisoners, and the under-trial females shall, if possible, be kept apart from the convicts. The female ward shall be so situated as not to be overlooked by any part of the male jail; and there shall be a separate hospital for sick female prisoners within or directly adjoining the female enclosure. They shall not be required to attend at the jail office. All enquiries and verification of their warrants shall be conducted by the Jailor in the female enclosure.[113]

Whatever might be the provisions for women prisoners, for their safety, the condition is not up to the satisfaction. The condition of women prisoners in Bangladesh is worsening day by day. The women are not safe either in the society due to torture perpetrated by the miscreants of the society or in the police custody or in prisons because of numerous reasons. The female prisoners are being subjected to the violation of their human rights through rape, molestation, and indecent behaviour by the members of the LEA. Even the safeguards provided by the Bengal Jail Code, because of their being female are not being provided to them. They are subject to all kinds of torture either physical or mental. Yasmin rape and murder case, the Sheema Chowdhury rape and murder case are the outstanding examples out of many by the members of the LEA.[114] Besides these, torture through beating and kicking has been one of the ordinary means of torture of the women accused by the LEA. Out of the fear of extreme torture, the female detainees are venturing the risk of running away from police custody at the dead of night. The following incident may be taken into consideration in this regard.

A woman of village Mulbari under Ghatail Police Station in Tangail district fled from the Police Station (PS) in apprehension of torture at midnight of 27 January in 1999. The victim was identified as Khodeza Khatun (37), wife of Abdus Salam of the above mentioned address. The husband of the victim and local people told the BRCT Fact-finding team on 11 July 1999 that police of Ghatail PS led by SI Mamun arrested his wife Khodeza Khatun at about 11.00 PM on 27 January 1999 on the charge of alleged kidnapping of a girl. Police broke the door of their house, entered into the room, kicked and beat Khodeza when she was alone in her house at that night. Police took her to the PS and could not put her in the female custody of the PS because both of the custodies of male and female were overcrowded. Police asked her to stay outside the custody. At the dead of night when Khodeza got the sentry slumbering, she managed to flee from the PS. BRCT conducted a Fact-finding mission on 10, 11 and 12 of July in 1999 following a report published in a Dhaka based daily news papers which alleged that Khodeza was killed by police and her dead body was concealed. The allegation of newspaper did not prove true while the husband of the victim, Abdus Salam, asserted that his wife had come back home after a lapse of more than five months.[115] So what is manifested by the above mentioned incident is that torture of every kind by the police is a trauma for the detainees both male and female alike.

Rape in police custody has been rampant in our country by the very policemen who are supposed to protect them from such torture. In 2000 members of the LEA raped seventeen women.[116] Again in jails, the women prisoners are treated as like as a male prisoner. The women prisoners are thrown into the police van after arrest where they have to go along with the male prisoners and no special measure for their carriage is taken to protect them from abuse. In Bangladesh, there is a scarcity of women Police Officer who are supposed to deal with the women prisoners. For this reason, within 24 hours of arrest, the women prisoners often get victimized by the middlemen who come in between the process to secure their release.[117]

Torture has not been limited to physical infliction only. The female prisoners of Bangladesh have to undergo mental torture due to the ill treatment of the members of the jail authority. Mental harassment is a constant picture of the jail inmate of Bangladesh. Severe mental torture is inflicted upon them. The inhuman mental torture can be pictured out through the following incident.

> "... one day a jail inmate, a young girl, received fried rice and chicken from her home through police. As a female warden saw her taking the food, she rushed to her and kicked the plate down. She hurled abuses at the girl in a very rude way. Unnerved by the abusive behaviour, the girl broke down in tears".[118]

This incident is not an isolated incident in the prisons of Bangladesh rather it has become a common picture for the jail inmates in Bangladesh. As human being prisoners deserve to get minimum congenial atmosphere in the prisons. It means that every prisoner male or female should have proper and adequate space facility, medical care and other necessities. Proper supply of food and drinking water should be ensured.

In this connection the provisions of the Bengal Jail Code say that,

> "In the female division of every jail there shall be a block of cells sufficient in number for use as punishment cells and to afford separate accommodation for female under-trial prisoners. A female under-trial prisoner may, at the option of the Superintendent, if cell accommodation is available, have the choice of occupying a cell in the female enclosure instead of being confined in the under-trial prisoners ward: provided the arrangements prescribed in Rule 954 regarding the guarding of cells in the female ward and the custody of the keys of these cells can be made."[119]

It is to be mentioned regretfully that the prisoners in Bangladesh suffer from lack of adequate space facility. They are not given enough space to satisfy the minimum requirement for health. Statistics collected from government and non-government organizations showed that the total capacity of the jails in the country is about 25,000; but now there are over 75,000 inmates in the prisons and accommodation available for female prisoners in countries (in 64 prisons) are 1051; but the number of inmates are 51700.[120] The picture of the plight of women prisoners in Bangladesh is that they are in inhuman condition in the prisons. To ensure the human rights of the women prisoners, adequate space facility should be provided to them.

The provisions of the Jail Code in this context are very clear. According to the Jail Code, no male officer shall have any entrance to any female prisoners enclosure and if unavoidably necessary, he may enter the same with company of any female warder. In this connection, the Jail Code provides that,

> "No male officer of the jail shall on any pretext enter the female prisoner's enclosure alone or unless he has a duty to attend to there. If a male officer has to attend to any duty in the females' enclosure and there is a paid matron or female warder, he may enter the females'

> enclosure in her company, and shall be accompanied by her to whatever part of the female jail he may have to go; if the matron is a convict, he shall be accompanied by a Head Warder, and the two shall not separate whilst in the females' enclosure at night, the Head Warder on duty shall call the Jailer, and these two officers together, shall enter the enclosure. Warders acting as escorts to official visitors must remain outside the enclosure while prisoners are being inspected".[121]

In the police stations the existing number of female Police Officer is insufficient to treat women prisoners. Though the provisions of the Jail Code very specifically deal with the issue that the women prisoners be totally secluded from the male prisoners, implementation of the said provisions is far beyond reality.

Privacy has to be maintained strictly and the wilful violation of this strictness is the violation of the guarantee as specified and endorsed by different national and international instruments.[122] The provisions of the Jail Code assert that the privacy of the female prisoners has to be strictly maintained and in no way it be whittled down. For the purpose of having foot prints, finger impressions of a female prisoner or to photograph or to measure her, she shall not be brought out of the enclosure and while doing so, the Police Officer and the Deputy Jailer or a Head Warder shall be in company of a matron or of the female convict warder or overseer in charge.[123]

Right to association is one of the basic human rights as loneliness is the cause of instrumental pain and may lead to mental disorder. This basic human right has also been guaranteed to the female prisoners. If there is only one female prisoner in the ward, she shall be allowed to enjoy the visit of her female friend. The Jail Code in this regard provides,

> When there is only one female prisoner in the female ward and there is no female warder, the Superintendent shall arrange to allow a female friend to visit the prisoner and live with her in the jail. If the female prisoner has no friend who will stay with her, the Superintendent shall entertain a female as an extra

warder to keep her company in anticipation of the Inspector-General's (IG Prison) sanction.[124]

Provisions have also been provided to protect the female prisoners from any sort of harassment by the male prisoners or the male staff of the jail. For this purpose it has been provided by the Jail Code that the keys of the female division shall be under the custody of the paid matron or female warder during the day and at night be under the custody of the Jailer and the keys shall remain in her custody until required next morning for the opening of the female wards.[125]

Again, for the maintenance of privacy it has been provided by the Jail Code that the locks of the female cells and wards shall be different from those in use in other parts of the jail and the same key shall not be used to unlock the other parts of the jail. The keys shall be under an old and trustworthy officer if there be no paid matron or female warder.[126]

Right to observe the religious institutions has been guaranteed as one of the fundamental rights in the Constitution of Bangladesh.[127] It has also been declared as one of the fundamental human rights in the UDHR.[128] The Constitution of Bangladesh provides freedom of religion. However, this right to observe the religious institutions has not been guaranteed by the Jail Code entirely. According to the provisions of the Jail Code, at the time of physical training the women prisoners are to remain bare head, hair flowing and with the upper part of the body covered with a *kurta* only.[129]

This is the direct violation of the provisions of Islam regarding the dress of the Muslim women. According to the tenets of Islam, women of adult age or women who have attained puberty shall maintain the strict principle relating to dress. Here, they have to cover their heads with scarf. But the provisions of Jail Code relating to parade of women prisoners express that they have to remain with bare head while they are in parade. This is a violation of the constitutionally guaranteed fundamental right and also the human right declared in the UDHR. However, it does not mean that the women prisoners are all the time asked to remain with bare head. Inside the prison cell, at all other time excluding that of necessary for parading, they are supplied with necessary wearing apparels and are allowed to maintain and observe their religious institutions.

The right to have proper dress meeting the demand of the seasons of Bangladesh, the female prisoners, like all other prisoners, are supplied with necessary wearing apparels under the provisions enumerating in Rule 1159 of the Jail Code. Rule 1159 dealt with the dress of all prisoners in division III sentenced to rigorous imprisonment while Rule 1165 deals with that of the convicted prisoners in division II sentenced to rigorous imprisonment.[130]

To enjoy the environment suitable for health and hygiene is another human right. This right has also been guaranteed by the Jail Code. As per the provisions of the Jail Code the hair of the female prisoners shall not be cut without the order of the Medical Officer where he considers this necessary on account of vermin or any disease. They are also supplied with comb and four necessary towels or napkins each.[131]

CONCLUSION

In prisons, most women come from poor families and with rural backgrounds. They mostly comprise of married, unmarried, divorced and estranged women involved in begging, odd jobs and prostitution. They are vulnerable to harassment and sexual abuse. When women and children of the country get various development opportunities for their development and empowerment, jails have been kept totally out of this development equation.[132] So, for the utmost and massive development of the country, the condition of the prisons should be improved. The prisoners should be treated as a member of whole human community. Otherwise a considerable portion of the total population will remain away from the light of human rights. It is a matter of hope that, the government in the recent years has been paying more attention about the condition of jail inmates and thinking of making some reformation in this regard.

NOTES

1. The 'right to a fair trial' in criminal cases or suits at law is ensured by Articles 10 and 11 of the UDHR and Article 14 of the ICCPR. Bangladesh as a state party of the ICCPR requires establishing a sufficient number of courts and tribunals and to regulate their procedure in a manner that at least fulfils the minimum guarantees set forth therein.
2. Nowak M, *UN Covenant on Civil and Political Rights: CCPR Commentary*, (Kehl: Engel Publishers, 1993), 241.
3. *Ibid.*
4. Report of 12 October 1978 in the *Zand Case*, D & R 15 (1979), 70.
5. *See*, General Assembly, Official Records, Fourteenth session, Annex (XIV), 34: Report of the Third Committee, A/4299 (3 December 1959), 6.
6. Communication No. 207/1986, para. 9.3; *See also* No. 289/1988, para. 6.6.
7. Communication No. 203/1986, para. 11.3, 12.
8. Concerning criminal proceedings, the HRC reiterated that 'the concept of a fair hearing necessarily entails that justice be rendered without undue delay' and consequently found violations of Article 14(1) and (3)(c) of the ICCPR.
9. English K and Stapleton A, *The Human Rights Handbook: A Practical Guide to Monitoring Human Rights* (Juta & Co. Ltd.: 1997), 48.
10. *Conteris vs. Uruguay*, Report of Forty-first session (A/41/40), annex VIII.C., para. 1.5.
11. *Gomez de Voituret vs. Uruguay*, Report. *Op. cit.*
12. Francis GJ, *The Europen Convention on Human Rights*, (Oxford, 1975), 102.
13. Appl. No. 434/58, *X vs. Sweden*, Yearbook II (1958-1959), 354; Appl. No. 8289/78, *X v. Austria*, D & R 18 (1980), 160.
14. Communication No. R. 7/22, Sala de touron, A/36/40, p. 120; Communication R. 17/70, Cubas, A/37/40,174
15. *Van Meurs vs. The Netherlands*, Report. *Op. cit.*, Forty-fifth Session (A/45/40), Vol. II. Annex IX.F.
16. *Constitution of Bangladesh*, Article 35(3) states that, "Every person accused of a criminal offence shall have the right to a speedy

and public trial by an independent and impartial court or tribunal established by law".

17. Report of 14 December 1979 in the case of *Le Compte, van Leuven and De Meyere, Paras.* 90-91.
18. See, *Caldas vs. Uruguay,* Report of the Human Rights Committee, Official Records of the General Assembly, *Forty-fifth Session* (A/45/40), Vol. II, annex IX. K.
19. *International Covenant on Civil and Political Rights (ICCPR),* Article 14(3)(c) states that, "every one shal! entitled to be tried without undue delay".
20. *See,* P. van Dijk and G.J.H van Hoof, *Theory and practice of the European Convention,* (Kluwer Deventer Publishers, 1983).
21. *See* Chapter 5.2.4 para. 2 and see also *supra note* 15.
22. AIR 1979, SC 1360; AIR 1979, SC 1369; *see* also Chapter....
23. AIR 1981 SC 1675.
24. Baxi U, 'Right to Speedy Trial geare, gander and Judicial Sauce (*State of Maharashtra vs. Champalal*)', 25 *J.I.L.I.* 90 at 105 (1983).
25. *See* Chapter 5.2.4 para. 2 and see also *supra note* 21.
26. Act No. XXVIII of 2002, Published in Bangladesh Gazette Extraordinary Dated 1 December 2002; *see also* 55 DLR (2003) 16
27. *The Speedy Trial Tribunal Act* 2002, Section 5.
28. *See* CCRP/C/SR. 56, p. 26 and CCRP/C/SR. 386, p. 5.
29. Earlier statements of the accused or of witnesses may also be used as elements of the evidence, provided that the accused is given ample opportunity, during the hearing, to revoke or refute them: *see* Appeal. No. 8414/78, *X vs. FRG,* D & R 17 (1980), 231 and Appeal No. 8417/78, *X v. Belgium,* D & R 16 (1979), 200
30. *Australia vs. Italy,* Yearbook VI (1963), 740.
31. Draft Principles, 10.
32. Draft Principles, 11.
33. Draft Principles, 11.
34. Hertzberg S and Zammuto C, *The Protection of Human Rights in the Criminal Process under International Instruments and National Constitutions,* (Sicily: 1981), 20.
35. *Montejo vs. Colombia,* Report. *Op. cit.,* Thirty-seventh Session (A/37/40), annex XV.

36. *Van Alphen vs. The Netherlands,* Report of the Forty-fifth Session (A/45/40), Vol.II. annex. IX.M.
37. *Ibid.*
38. *Bolanos vs. Ecuador,* Report. *Op. cit.,* Forty-fourth session (A/44/40), annex XIX.
39. Six years for murder trial, accused in detention, case still pending; For more information *see also,* Harris DJ, *Cases and Materials on International Law,* (Sweets & Maxwell: London) p. 674.
40. *Ibid.*
41. *International Covenant on Civil and Political Rights* 1966, Article 6.
42. English K and Stapleton A, *supra note* 9 at 25.
43. *The Daily Inqilab,* Dhaka (Bangladesh), 27 July 1999. The website of the *Daily Inqilab* is: *<http://www.dailyinqilab.com>*
44. *International Covenant on Civil and Political Rights (ICCPR)* 1966, Article 7.
45. *Constitution of Pakistan,* Article 14 (2).
46. *Constitution of Bangladesh,* Article 35 (5).
47. Annual Report of BRCT, 1996, *State of Human Rights,* Dhaka.
48. *See also* Chapter 2.7.
49. *Human Rights Fact-Finder,* (BRCT, Dhaka: March-April, 1997).
50. Annual Report of BRCT, 1997.
51. *Constitution of Bangladesh,* Article 27.
52. *Constitution of Bangladesh,* Article 33 (1).
53. *Constitution of Bangladesh,* Article 35(1) and the *Universal Declaration of Human Rights* 1948, Article 11(2).
54. *Constitution of Bangladesh,* Article 35(2).
55. *Constitution of Bangladesh,* Article 35(3) and the *Universal Declaration of Human Rights* 1948, Article 10.
56. *Constitution of Bangladesh,* Article 35(4).
57. *Constitution of Bangladesh,* Article 35(5) and the *Universal Declaration of Human Rights* 1948, Article 5.
58. Sharma PD, *Police and Criminal Justice Administration in India,* (1985), 145.
59. Paranjape NV, *Criminology and Penology,* (Ninth edition, 1996: Central Law Publication, Allahabad, India), 244.

60. *Bengal Jail Code* 1894, Chapter I.
61. *Prisons Act,* 1894 (Act No. IX of 1894), Section 3.
62. *Acosta vs. Uruguay,* Report of the Thirty-ninth Session (A/39/40), annex. XI.
63. Annual Report of BRCT (May-June issue, 1997), *State of Human Rights,* p. 50; *see also* Chapter 2.7.
64. *The Prisons Act* 1894, Section 56.
65. AIR 1980 SC 1579; (1980) 3 SCC 488.
66. AIR 1978 SC 1675; (1734, 1735), (1978) 4 SCC 494, 1978 Cr.L.J. 1741.
67. *Pratt and Morgan vs. Jamaica,* Report, *Op. cit.,* Forty-fourth Session (A/44/40), annex X.F.
68. *Pinto vs. Trinidad and Tobago,* Report of the HRC Official Records of the General Assembly, Forty-fifth Session (A/45/40), Vol. II. Annexe IX H.
69. *Gilboa vs. Uruguay,* Report of the Forty-first session (A/41/40), annex VIII B
70. (1985) 2 Selected Decisions of HRC 151 at 154; see also, *Kelly vs. Jamaica* (1997) 4 IHRR. 334.
71. General Comment 13 (Twenty-first session, 1984) [See 19 UNGAOR, Supp No. 40 (A/39/40 and Corr. 1 and 2) annex VI).
72. A/C, 3/L. 795/Rev. 3; A/C, 3/SR, 967.
73. *See,* DCE Doc. H (70) 7, 38.
74. This was ascertained in several cases against Uruguay, in which a defence counsel was appointed *ex officio* by the military courts; *see,* e.g., Nos. 52, 56/1979; No. 73/1980.
75. *See,* e.g. Nos. 6, 8/1977; Nos. 28, 32/1978, Nos. 49, 63/1979, Nos. 70, 73, 74, 80, 83/1980, Nos. 92, 103, 110/1981; Nos. 123, 124/1982; No. 139/1983, Nos. 283, 289,338/1988, *see* McGoldrick D, 422; & TREAT.
76. Sarker AH, *Criminology: Theory and Analysis,* Kollol Prokashony, Dhaka: 2005), 229.
77. Annual Report of BRCT, 1997, *State of Human Rights,* (published in 1997: Dhaka), 52.
78. Roy Nirmolendu, 'Jail Code: Status and Right of prisoners and Situation of Human Rights in the prisons', in *Human Rights Law,* (Dhaka: 1997); *See also* Manobadhikar, Dhaka, 31 August 1999.

79. A renowned weekly in Bangladesh.
80. Annual Report of BRCT, 1999, *State of Human Rights,* Dhaka, 12.
81. Annual Report of BRCT, 2000, *State of Human Rights,* Dhaka, 10.
82. *The Prothom Alo,* Dhaka (Bangladesh), 8 September 2001. The website of the *Daily Prothom Alo* is: <*http://www.prothom-alo.com*>.
83. *Bangladeshe Kishore Aparadher Bichar Babostha O' Shishuder Biruddha Sohingsota Songkronto Borshopunji* (The judicial system of Juvenile offences and Annual Report regarding violence against children in Bangladesh), Save the Children, UK and Odhikar: 2001), 30.
84. Chowdhury AH, 'Jail Situation, 1995', in *State of Human Rights, 1997,* (Manobadhikar, Dhaka: 31 July 1999).
85. Annual Report of BRCT, 1998, *State of Human Rights,* Dhaka, 14.
86. At present there are 9 central jails and 55 are district jails in Bangladesh
87. *The Daily Star,* Dhaka (Bangladesh), 23 June 2000.
88. *Ibid.*
89. *Ibid.*
90. *The Bengal Jail Code* 1894, Chapter XV, Rule 616.
91. *The Bengal Jail Code* 1894, Chapter XL, Section II, Rule 1231.
92. See, *supra note* 74 at 24.
93. Annual Report of BRCT, (Dhaka: 1992), *State of Human Rights,* Dhaka, 48.
94. *Bangladeshe Kishore Aparadher Bichar Babostha O' Shishuder Biruddha Sohingsota Songkronto Borshopunji* (The judicial system of Juvenile offences and Annual Report regarding violence against children in Bangladesh), Save the Children, UK and Odhikar: 2001), (Save the Children, UK and Odhikar: 2005), 24.
95. *Human Rights Law* 1997, (Dhaka: 1997), 339.
96. *Ibid.*
97. *State of Human Rights,* 1991-1997; *Human Rights Fact-finder,* 1997; *Annual Report, 1998,* (BRCT, Dhaka), 15.
98. Annual Report of BRCT, 1998, *State of Human Right,* Dhaka, 14.
99. Annual Report of BRCT, 2000, *State of Human Rights,* Dhaka, 10.

100. *The Bengal Jail Code* 1894, Chapter-XVI, Rules 633, 634.
101. *The Bengal Jail Code,* Chapter - XL, Section I, Rules 1214.
102. Das JA, 'Condition of Prison and Rights of Prisoners', in *Human Rights in Bangladesh 2001,* Ain O' Salish Kendra (ASK), Dhaka: 2002.
103. Interviews have been made with the Prisoners in the Rajshahi Central Jail and in the Rajshahi Sessions Court while the Prisoners were produced in the court. Interviews have also been made with the prisoners in Kushtia, Pabna, Comilla and Chittagong, the findings was similar and therefore this interview reflects the jail situation of Bangladesh.
104. *See* the Questionnaire Form in Appendix VII.
105. AIR 1966 SC 424.
106. AIR 1971 SC 2092.
107. AIR 1978 SC 1675.
108. AIR 1979 SC 1819; *See also* Chapter 5.2.6.
109. AIR 1983 SC 378.
110. *Sanjay Suri vs. Delhi Administration,* CrLJ (1988) 705 (SC).
111. Rem Pal Singh, 'Yoga and Indian Penology' in *Central Indian Law Quarterly Journal,* Vol. 1(1987), 92-93.
112. Paranjape NV, *Criminology and Penology,* (Ninth edition, Central Law Publications, Allahabad: 1996), 269.
113. *The Bengal Jail Code* 1894, Rule 945.
114. *See,* Chapter 2.7 and *see also* Chapter 5.5.2.
115. Bangladesh Rehabilitation Centre for Trauma Victims (BRCT), *Annual Report* 1999, 21.
116. Bangladesh Rehabilitation Centre for Trauma Victims (BRCT), *Annual Report* 2000, 9.
117. *Ibid.*
118. *The Daily Star,* Dhaka (Bangladesh), 25 August 2002.
119. *The Bengal Jail Code* 1894, Rule 946.
120. *The Daily Star,* Dhaka (Bangladesh), 25 August 2002.
121. *The Bengal Jail Code* 1894, Rule 950.
122. *Constitution of Bangladesh,* Article 43 and the *Universal Declaration of Human Rights* 1948, Article 12.

123. *The Bengal Jail Code* 1894, Rule 951.
124. *The Bengal Jail Code 1892,* Rule 948.
125. *The Bengal Jail Code* 1894, Rule 952.
126. *The Bengal Jail Code* 1894, Rule 953f.
127. *Constitution of Bangladesh,* Article 41.
128. *Universal Declaration of Human Rights* 1948, Article 18.
129. *The Bengal Jail Code*1894, Rule 956; For clothing to be supplied to female prisoners *see,* Rules 1159 and 1165.
130. A list of dress of the women prisoners is given in Appendix VII.
131. *The Bengal Jail Code* 1894, Rule 960.
132. *The Daily Star,* Dhaka (Bangladesh), 25 August 2002.

INTERVIEWS WITH THE ACCUSED AND DIFFERENT OFFICIALS

6

INTRODUCTION

243 persons[1] of several police stations of 8 districts namely, Dhaka, Rajshahi, Chittagong, Barishal, Comilla, Jessore, Faridpur and Jhenaidah were interviewed from the lists received from police stations on random basis on different aspects of violation of human rights. We received information from them regarding the nature of violation of human rights including the treatment they received from the executives under police or jail custody or during remand. Besides, 16 lawyers, 52 judicial officers and 54 Police Officers were interviewed in order to obtain their opinion regarding the state of human rights in Bangladesh. The study reveals that human rights have been and are being violated by the executives in the banner of black law like the Special Powers Act, 1974 or under the coverage of anti-human provisions of different Codes prevalent in Bangladesh. Illegal detention under the Special Powers Act, misuse of Sections 54 and 167 of the Cr. P. C. contribute to a large extent in violating human rights in the country. This has been shown in a tabular form:

INTERVIEWS WITH VICTIMS

Victims of violation of human rights both by the Law Enforcing Agencies (LEA) and by others. Table shows the percentage of violation of human rights by LEA and others.

Table 1

Victim of violation of human rights by LEA	*Victim of violation of human rights by others*	*Not responding*	*Total*
222 (93.27%)	16 (6.72%)	5	243 (100%)

243 persons have been interviewed of whom 222 persons became the victim of violation of human rights by the LEA like police, jail authority; 16 persons became the victim of such violation by persons other than LEA and 5 persons did not answer in this respect.

Violation has been divided into two categories, physical and mental. Table shows these two types of violation:

Table 2

Physical torture	*Mental torture*	*Total*
147 (66.21)	75 (33.78)	222 (100%)

222 persons were interviewed of them 147 persons were physically tortured and 75 persons were tortured mentally.

The following table shows the place where human rights have been violated.

Table 3

Jail custody	*Police custody*	*Both jail and police custody*	*Total*
48 (21.62%)	168 (75.67%)	6 (2.70%)	222 (100%)

It has been stated earlier that violation of human rights under jail and police custody sometimes led to death of the victims.

Violation of Human Rights under SPA and Others Laws

Out of 243 persons 225 persons detained/arrested under the Special Powers Act and by other laws shown in the following table.

Table 4

Under the SPA	*By other laws*	*Sub-total*	*Not applicable*	*Total*
73 (32.44%)	152 (67.55%)	225 (100%)	18	243

Out of 243 persons interviewed 73 persons were detained under the SPA, 152 persons were kept in custody in the jail and 18 persons do not fall under any category.

Table 5
Period of Detention under the SPA

30 day	*30 days to 90 days*	*120 days*	*121 days to 180 days*	*More than 180 days*	*Total*
16	19	16	13	09	73

Out of 243 persons who were interviewed 73 persons were detained by the SPA. 16 persons were detained for 30 days, 19 persons were detained up to 90 days, 16 persons were detained up to 120 days, 13 persons were detained up to 180 days and 9 persons were detained from 240 days up to a maximum period of 34 months.

Table 6
Arrested Persons Taken under Remand and Otherwise

Remanded	*Without remand*	*Sub-total*	*Not applicable*	*Total*
88 (39.11%)	137 (60.88%)	225 (100%)	18	243

Out of 243 persons interviewed 88 persons were granted remand by the Magistrate, which is, 39.11% and 137 persons were not taken into remand which is 60.88%. Rest of the18 persons do not fall in any category.

This table shows how the persons detained/arrested tried to get relief from torture by giving bribe to the police authority or by using political influence during remand.

Table 7

Bribe given	*Political influence used*	*Not applicable*	*Total*
52 (60%)	05 (5.68%)	31	88 (100%)

The above table shows that 88 persons were taken into remand under Section 167 of the Cr. P. C. out of 243 persons interviewed. 60% of the remanded persons were forced to pay bribe to the police authority and 5.68% used political influence in order to get relief from physical and mental torture. This shows the nature of violation of human rights during remand, although there is constitutional bar against torture either during remand or otherwise.

Statement given by one of the 88 accused arrested is stated herein below to reveal the nature of torture by police under their custody.

Moulana Motahar Hossain, now a local College teacher of Rajshahi town, was arrested by Boalia thana police under Rajshahi district while performing *maghrib* prayer at Hatemkhan Mosque on 14 June 1997. In the police station he was beaten mercilessly by 4 police personnel by turn. He was kicked by boot and hit by helmet on his head. He was not supplied with water to quench his thirst, though later on it was given. On 15 June he was taken in a small room where his eyes were clothed. Thereafter he was given electric shock and in consequence he lost sense. He was then sent to Rajshahi Central Jail where he became seriously ill due to electric shock and physical torture. His heart was affected and so he was sent to Rajshahi Medical College Hospital in cardiology ward from were he was sent to Dhaka PG Hospital when his condition further deteriorated. He was then confined for 39 days to jail where he was not given proper diet, kept under bar fetter (Dandaberi). Bail petition was refused several times. But ultimately he was granted bail by Sessions' Judge Court after 38 days. He has not still fully cured from cardiatic problem, which is the effect of electric shock when this report was finally written in 2000.

Another victim, Sarwar Kamal, a student of Law Department of Rajshahi University, was arrested twice by Motihar thana police under Rajshahi district without warrant. He was first arrested on 25 November 1997 and for the second time on 13 February 1998 from Sher-E-Bangla Hall, Rajshahi University. He stated in the interview that both the times he was tortured physically by the police of Motihar thana as a part of their routine work and as a result of such torture one of his ankle was fractured. He was also taken into remand for 4 days where he was both physically and mentally tortured. He was not given cloth to cover his body to protect from cold, though it was winter and he fell ill. But no medical care was taken. He was then sent to Rajshahi Central Jail where he was kept confined for three months. There he received inadequate food, inadequate space to sleep and inhuman behaviour from the jail authority, as he did not give any bribe to them for release.

Another victim of violation of human rights is M. A. Hannan, a student of Islamic University, Kushtia. He was arrested by the Kushtia Police Station under Kushtia district on 31 October 1993. In the interview he stated that he was tortured by Kushtia thana police inhumanly and mercilessly. Thereafter he was sent to Kushtia District Jail where he was not given proper medical treatment. He led an inhuman life for 63 days in the jail.

Md. Isharat Ali, an under trial prisoner was in Pabna district Jail for 3 months and 15 days from December 1994 to March 1995. He was a businessman who held the position of Upazila Chairman of Atgharia. His bail hearing was delayed for this long time for political rivalry. He said that the meal of the jail, the condition of the room and the process of meeting with the relatives were not satisfactory. He added that the behaviour of the prison police was not good. He had to stay in a small room with another 50 to 60 prisoners. Due to this congestion he could hardly sleep peacefully for all this time. At last he granted bail and later he was acquitted from the case.

Of the 243 persons interviewed, 98% replied that there were no lawful grounds for their detention/arrest.

Table 8
Violation of Human Rights under Jail Custody

Victim of violation of human rights	*No Victim of violation of human rights*	*Total*
210 (46.41%)	33 (13.58)	243 (100%)

Table shows that 46.41% prisoners are the victims of violation of human rights.

Table 9
Statistics of Bail Granted by Different Courts

Magistrate Courts	*Sessions Court*	*High Court Divisions of Supreme Court*	*Bail rejected*	*Total*
115 (4356%)	90 (34%)	49 (15.56%)	10 (3.78%)	264 (100%)

Of 243 persons, 21 persons were arrested more than one and as such the total number has become 264 (243+21). Table shows that 43.56% arrested persons were granted bail by Magistrate Courts, 34% by sessions courts, 18.56% by High Court Division of Supreme Court and 3.78% (10 arrested) were not granted bail up to the time when they were interviewed. It is to be noted that the bail petition of most of the arrested persons were rejected several times even in some cases it was rejected for thirty times.

INTERVIEWS WITH LAWYERS

16 lawyers were interviewed regarding the causes of violation of human rights. Opinion about preventive detention, its legal foundation and also their concern about the repeal of the SPA and amendment of Section 54 of the Cr. P. C.

Table 7
Causes of Violation of Human Rights

Absence of proper application of law	*Misuse of power by*	*Unusual delay in disposing of suit*	*Abuse of power by LEA*	*Total*
12	×	×	4 (+2)	16

Table shows that out of 16 legal practitioners 12 said that the cause of violation of human rights in Bangladesh is the absence of proper execution of law, 4 said that both absence of proper execution of law and abuse of power by LEA are responsible for violation of human rights.

Table 8
Opinion About Preventive Detention under the SPA

Inhuman	*Days Violation of human rights*	*Harassment*	*Total*
5 (41.66%)	5 (41.66%)	02 (16.66%)	12 (100%)

41.66% said that preventive detention is inhuman, 41.66% said that it is violation of human rights and 16.66% that it is nothing but harassment.

16 lawyers were interviewer regarding the causes of human rights violation. Table shows the statistics indicating the causes of violation.

Table 9

Absence of proper application of law	*Misuse of power by*	*Unusual delay in disposing of suit*	*Abuse of power by LEA*	*Total*
12	–	–	4	16

Out of 16 lawyers 12 said that the cause of violation of human rights is absence of proper application of law, 4 lawyers opined that both absence of proper application of law and abuse of power by LEA are responsible for violation of human rights.

Table 10
Opinion about Preventive Detention under the SPA

Inhuman	*Violation of human rights*	*Harassment*	*Total*
6 (41.66%)	6 (41.66%)	4 (16.66%)	16 (100%)

41.66% said that preventive detention is inhuman, 41.66% said that it is violation of human rights and 16.66% that it is nothing but harassment.

Table 11
Legal Foundation of Torture Under Remand and Opinion of Lawyers about Granting Remand

Legal	*No legal foundation*	*Total*
x	16 (100%)	16 (100%)

100% lawyers expressed their opinion against police remand 100% lawyers also said that confinement of an accused in the jail for an indefinite period due to procedural complicacy is unjustifiable and amounts to violation of human rights.

Opinion regarding amendment or repeal of Sections 54 and 167 of the Cr. P. C. and SPA.

Table 12

In favour of amendment of Sections 54 and 167	*In favour of repeal of SPA*	*Total*
6 (41.66%)	10 (100%)	16 (100%)

41.66% want amendment of Sections 54 and 167 of the Cr. P. C. and 90% want the repeal of the SPA. Some of them opined that no need to repeal the provisions of these 2 Sections, but there should be proper guidelines and appropriate measures in the application of those provisions.

INTERVIEWS WITH JUDICIAL OFFICERS

We interviewed 52 judicial officers of Rajshahi, Dhaka, Barisal, Faridpur, Khulna, Chittagong, Jessore and Jhenidah in order to get idea regarding the state of human rights of the accused during or in course of trial and also the impacts of Section 54 of Cr. P. C. and SPA upon the accused/detainees or convicts.

Where any accused became the victim of discrimination during trial:

Table 13

Victim of discrimination	*No discrimination*	*Abstained*	*Total*
6 (11.53%)	42 (80.76%)	4 (7.69%)	52 (100%)

Out 52 judicial officers, 6 said that in some cases discrimination takes place, 42 said no discrimination takes place and rest 4 abstained from making any comment.

Comments of the judicial officers regarding amendment of Sections 54 and 167 of the Cr. P. C.

Table 14

In favour of amendment	*Not in favour of amendment*	*Abstained*	*Total*
13 (25%)	34 (65.38%)	5 (9.61%)	52 (100%)

25% is in favour of amendment of Sections 54 and 164 of the Cr. P. C whereas 65.38% against amendment of those sections, rest 9.61% abstained from making any remark.

INTERVIEWS WITH POLICE OFFICERS

54 Police Officers were interviewed in order to receive their opinion about remand, detention, physical and mental torture of the accused or detainees during remand.

Table 15

Arguments in favour of granting remand	*Against granting remand*	*Total*
26 (48%)	28 (52%)	54 (100%)

48% police officers opined that in order to get information from the accused remand is necessary, whereas 52% gave opinion against remand.

Table 16
Opinion Regarding Detention

Justification of detention	*Against detention*	*Abstained*	*Total*
34 (62.96%)	17 (31.48%)	3 (5.55%)	54 (100%)

34 Police Officer argued in favour of detention whereas 17 argued against detention. 3 Officers abstained from making any comment.

Table 17
Effects on Human Rights for Delay in Disposal of Suits

Delay in disposing of suit amounts to violation of human rights	*Not violation of human rights*	*Abstained*	*Total*
12 (22.22%)	34 (62.96%)	8 (14.81%)	54 (100%)

22.22% police officer said that delay in disposing of suit leads to violation of human rights 62.96% opined that delay does not amount to violation of human rights, 14.81% abstained from making any comment.

CONCLUSION

In this study it was attempted to take interview of 50 judicial officers, 50 members of the LEA and 50 Lawyers. But the interview was made of 52 judicial officers, 54 members of LEA and 16 Lawyers. Though the number of Lawyers is not fulfilled to 50 most of them are renowned lawyers of the Supreme Court of Bangladesh having good records on this particular issue and therefore opinion of them consciously reflects the original picture of the matter concerned.

In this empirical study for assessing the actual situation of the human rights of the accused, reliance was made on interviews of the victims or accused along with different personnel mentioned above. Though there exists a dissenting opinion among their views, the study reveals a clear picture of violation of human rights in the country.

Since the provisions of Sections 54 and 167 of the Cr. P. C. and the SPA are the necessary evils in the context of Bangladesh, some of the interviews suggest for repeal whereas some other prescribe for bringing reform in those laws and fair application thereof.

NOTE

1. Political persons 03, Teachers 08, Advocates 01, Students 112, Business man 56, Service holder 14, Unemployed persons 09, Farmer 25, Labour 13, Hawker 01 and Beggar 01.

GENERAL CONCLUSIONS 7

INTRODUCTION

The study on human rights has become a widely discussed subject all over the world. As human rights are inalienable, inviolable and above all essential to human life, its protection and promotion have received a new dimension and momentum by the governments as well as by the human rights activists. As human rights are birth-rights, these are to be enjoyed by every human being from birth to death without any interference either by public or by private individual. It is a reality that violations of human rights are being committed more or less in almost all the countries of the world. Bangladesh is not an exception to this.[1]

The foregoing discussions reveal that from 1945 to date more than sixty human rights instruments either in the form of a declaration or in the form of a convention or a covenant have been adopted by the UN with a view to prevent human rights violations and to promote and protect human rights internationally. Only a few of those important instruments have been explained in order to study their effectiveness and the role of the concerned organisation for promoting and protecting human rights. In fact, the sincerity of the world body, effective co-operation of the states, impartial implementation of the provisions of the human rights instruments are the determinants for prevention of violation and protection and promotion of human rights. Although UN and its subordinate organisations related to human rights are active for preventing human rights violations in different parts of the world, and they have become successful to some extent, still it can be said without any hesitation that violations have not been stopped due to non-cooperation of the states concerned where such violations are being committed. Besides, ethnic and political differences, ideological conflict between the states or between the groups within the state are additional factors for such violations. It is evident in Algeria, Afghanistan, Palestine, Bosnia and Kosovo that human rights violations have been daily affairs. Human rights and fundamental freedoms, however, are birthrights and not mercy from any quarter. So their promotion and protection is the primary responsibility of the governments concerned.

It is a fact that international organisations, governmental as well as non-governmental, both local and foreign, are more active and aware than before for the protection and promotion of human rights. At the beginning of 21st century human rights have received fuller recognition nationally and internationally. Now it is essential that effective mechanism is incorporated so that all the states of the world can strictly follow and observe the provisions of international instruments on human rights. The states as well as the governments must be made accountable in case of violation of these rights in their territories.

Besides, the most effective ways and means for the protection of human rights, it is submitted, is that the victims of violation of human rights must be organised to protest against such violations so that the violators will be morally weakened and the oppressed will morally boost up and thereby activate world opinion in favour of the oppressed. The days are ahead when people will be more conscious of their rights, as guaranteed in different international human rights instruments and will be more organised for the protection and promotion of their rights.

The rights of the accused being eventually part of the human rights strategy must necessarily be recognised by the constitution and the law of every country to safeguard the individual's personal liberty against the autocracy and authoritarianism of the Government.[2] Therefore, the principle that every person is to be presumed innocent until proved guilty by the court dominates the criminal jurisprudential philosophy of both in international law and laws of Bangladesh. Running parallel to the principle is another extremely vital principle, which requires that the burden of proving the guilt of the accused beyond all reasonable doubt should be placed on the prosecution. On the basis of the aforementioned irrefutable principles of criminal jurisprudence the Law-making body of Bangladesh has incorporated in the Constitution and criminal legislation a series of provisions with the object of safeguarding the interests of the accused. These provisions that have been defined as basic human rights of the individual in any civilised order have been examined and analysed in the present study. Thus, the findings of the study can be summed up in terms of significant rights as follows:

FINDINGS OF THE STUDY

In Bangladesh enjoyment of human rights face a serious set back both by the LEA like police, BDR and Ansar and private elements like *Mastan,* terrorists, smugglers, rapists etc. The study reveals that there are lots of factors responsible for the violation of human rights. In most of the cases, LEA are directly or indirectly involved for such violation. If the LEA specially the police, discharged their duties sincerely, violation of human rights would have reduced to a large extent. The study further reveals that the presence of anti humanitarian law, misuse of powers by executives are no less responsible for violation of human rights. Efforts have been made to find out the causes of such violation and remedial measures against such violation have also been suggested in previous chapters.

The Constitution of Bangladesh guarantees fundamental human rights. In spite of that, sometimes the accused and convicts under police or jail custody become the victim of violation of human rights. It is unfortunate that there are many incidents of physical and mental torture upon the innocent persons by police and jail authority in order to extract bribe from them. We received information through interviews from

243 civilians, some judicial officers, some police officers and also legal practitioners regarding the state of human rights. Majority of them (243 persons) stated that they become the victim of violation of human rights. Statement of under trial prisoners, detainees reflect that they also become the violation of human rights.

The misuse of Sections 54 and 167 of the Cr. P. C,[3] the arbitrary detention under the coverage of the SPA, torture by police during remand, poor and unhealthy condition of prison, rape of female detainees in prison, electric shock during police custody, arbitrary arrest of the activists of opposition political parties have become a very normal affairs in Bangladesh. National dailies, weeklies, human rights journals of Bangladesh and even human rights practices published by US Department of State highlight the nature of violation of human rights in Bangladesh.[4]

RECOMMENDATIONS AND GUIDELINES FOR REFORM

In this study the enumerated findings and conclusions lead us to make certain suggestions to effect reforms in the legal framework with a view to better achieving human rights of the accused. The present suggestions would mainly relate to the Bangladeshi legal system, which could emulate worthwhile features from the international system as well.

In the light of the viewpoint of governments, it would be desirable to consider ways by which the right to a fair trial might be strengthened, for example, by making the right to a fair trial or certain aspects of the right non-derogable. In that regard the study would consider the elaboration of a Third Optional Protocol to the ICCPR, which would add Article 14 related to the right to a fair trial provision to the list of provisions, which cannot be derogated from Article 4 of the Covenant. It would also be desirable to consider other means of strengthening the implementation of the right to a fair trial.

The Government of Bangladesh must pay heed to protect the rights of the accused, convicts and members of the public by taking necessary security measures against the violators specially against LEA by establishing more courts and appointing more judges for speedy and impartial trial. Besides, Sections 54, 167 and 344 of the Cr. P. C. must be amended in order to stop torture committed by police in the name of remand. Police very often misuse the application of Section 54 and maliciously arrest innocent persons in order to claim bribe from them. A number of such cases have been stated in previous chapters.[5] The study reveals that police is directly or indirectly responsible for committing major offences in the country. It is also revealed that the misapplication of the SPA is another cause for repression and illegal detention.

The UN General Assembly, with a view to protect and promote the human rights of the accused and fundamental freedoms, made a clarion call to the States in the Declaration on the Right to Development, 1986 as follows:[6]

> All human rights and fundamental freedoms are indivisible and interdependent; equal attention and urgent consideration should be given to the implementation, promotion and protection of civil, economic, social and cultural rights.

It is worth noting that Bangladesh has already acceded to the ICCPR considered by the human rights experts as the most influential human rights mechanism of the UN. Through this ratification Bangladesh has undertaken to respect and to ensure all individuals within its territory and subject to its jurisdiction the rights recognized in the Covenant without any discrimination irrespective of race, sex, colour, language, age, religion etc. It may be significant to mention here that after five years of ratification it has still not incorporated the salient features of the Covenant into its municipal laws.

The Constitution of Bangladesh, no doubt, guarantees justiciable fundamental rights basic to democracy and worth of the individual but it does not protect specifically certain inalienable human rights enshrined in the ICCPR which are very vital for the defence of the accused in Bangladesh. They are the right to privacy, right to a fair trial, right against cruel and unusual punishment[7] and safeguards against excessive bail.

Repeal of black laws and sections, honest discharge of duties by the LEA, speedy trial and punishment of the violations of human rights, special security measures for women and children etc. may help to prevent violation of human rights in Bangladesh. However, we recommend the following specific steps for the promotion and protection of human rights in Bangladesh.[8]

1. Sections 54, 167, 344 of the Cr. P. C. should be amended in such a manner that scope of violation of human rights by police personnel cannot take place.
2. The SPA should be amended so that arbitrary detention granted by the executives will be prevented.
3. Medical examination of the arrested persons before and after remand is to be recorded.
4. Confession by the accused is to be made voluntarily before a Magistrate.
5. Investigation department should be separated from the police department where police is accused.
6. Police are to be trained on behavioural science for the development of human manner of the police personnel.
7. Police personnel should be trained on human rights.
8. Relevant law should be legislated to prevent torture or inhuman punishment as per Constitution of Bangladesh and the Convention Against Torture and other Cruel, Inhuman or Degrading Treatment or Punishment adopted by the UN General Assembly.
9. Honest persons and persons of high moral character should be appointed in the police department.
10. Parliamentary Human Rights Committee and National Human Rights Commission should be formed immediately to monitor and supervise the activities of the police.
11. Ombudsman should be appointed.
12. Women and children should be sent to reformation centres instead of jail.

13. Adequate compensation should be paid to the victim of violation of human rights and law should be legislated with this aim in view.
14. Human Rights should be included in the curriculum of School, College and University in order to make the students aware of it.
15. Relation between police and citizen should be improved for the protection and promotion of human rights.
16. International Bill of Human Rights and other UN documents on human rights should be ratified by the Government for implementation.
17. Exemplary punishment should be inflicted on the violators of human rights in a conspicuous place so that people can observe it and take lesson from it.
18. Summary trial should be held to expedite judicial system so that large backlog of case cannot take place. Sufficient number of courts should be established and the number of judicial officers should be increased for quick disposal of suits.
19. Number of prisons should be increased in order to accommodate the prisoners properly.
20. Staffs of jail should be so trained that they perform their public duty professionally and ethically.
21. Moral training is to be given to the inmates of jail so that they lead a moral life during and after jail life.
22. The last but not the least recommendation for the protection of human rights is orientation courses to ensure sense of accountability among the executives.
23. The oppressed and tortured persons should raise their voice against the oppressors. The Human Rights NGO can play a vital role in this respect.

If these recommendations are implemented, it is expected, the protection of human rights will be ensured and we can get a society free from lawlessness resulting in peaceful existence of people of varied race, colour, sex, religion and political difference.

NOTES

1. Ud-Din MF, and Hannan M. A., 'Protection of Human Rights in Criminal Justice: Bangladesh Perspective', *Research Project*, 1998, (Rajshahi University: 1998), 166; *see also* Chapter 1.4 and 3.9
2. Batra, M, *Protection of Human Rights in Criminal Justice Administration*, (Deep & Deep Publications, New Delhi: 1989), 131.
3. *Code of Criminal Procedure*, 1898, Act No V of 1898
4. United States Information Service (USIS), Dhaka published a report on the state of human rights in Bangladesh in 1999.
5. *See* Chapter 2.3.1 and 2.6.
6. *UN Declaration on the Right to Development* 1986, Article 6(2).
7. *International Covenant on Civil and Political Rights (ICCPR)* 1966, Articles 23, 20 and 9.
8. Most of the suggestions have been recommended in the *Article 5* (a News Letter of the Bangladesh Rehabilitation Centre for Trauma Victims (BRCT), Dhaka] during October to December, 1999.

APPENDICES

Relevant Provisions of the Constitution of Bangladesh

Relevant Provisions of the Fundamentals of the Code of Criminal Procedure (Cr. P. C.) in Bangladesh

Relevant Provisions of the Special Powers Act (SPA) in Bangladesh

Relevant Provisions of the Universal Declaration of Human Rights (UDHR)

Relevant Provisions of the International Covenant on Civil and Political Rights (ICCPR)

A list of dress for the Women Prisoners

APPENDIX-I
CONSTITUTION OF BANGLADESH

Relevant Provisions

Article 26: Laws Inconsistent with Fundamental Rights to be Void

(1) All existing law inconsistent with the provisions of this Part shall, to the extent of such inconsistency, become void on the commencement of this constitution.

(2) The state shall not make any law inconsistent with any provisions of this Part, and any law so made shall, to the extent of such inconsistency, be void.

(3) Nothing in this article shall apply to any amendment of this protection of law.

Article 27: Equality Before Law

All citizens are equal before law and are entitled to equal protection of law.

Article 31: Right to Protection of Law

To enjoy the protection of the law, and to be treated in accordance with law, and only in accordance with law, is the inalienable right of every citizen, whenever he may be, and of every other person for the time being within Bangladesh, and in particular no action detrimental to the life, liberty, body, reputation or property of any person shall be taken except in accordance with law.

Article 32: Protection of Right to Life and Personal Liberty

No person shall be derived of life or personal liberty save in accordance with law.

Article 33: Safeguards as to Arrest and Detention

(1) No person who is arrested shall be detained in custody without being informed, as soon as may be, of the grounds for such arrest, nor shall be denied the right to consult and be defended by a legal practitioner of his choice.

(2) Every person who is arrested and detained in custody shall be produced before the nearest Magistrate within a period of twenty-four hours of such arrest, excluding the time necessary for the

journey from the place of arrest to the court of the magistrate, and no such person shall be detained in custody beyond the said period without the authority of a Magistrate.

(3) Nothing in clauses (1) and (2) shall apply to any person–

(a) who for the time being is an enemy alien; or

(b) who is arrested or detained under any law providing for preventive detention

(4) No law providing for preventive detention shall authorise the detention of a person for a period exceeding six months unless an Advisory Board consisting of three persons, of whom two shall be persons who are, or have been, or are qualified to be appointed as, Judges of the Supreme Court and the other shall be a person who is a senior officer in the service of the Republic, has, after affording him an opportunity of being heard in person, reported before the expiration of the said period of six months that there is, in its opinion, sufficient cause for such detention.

(5) When any person is detained in pursuance of an order made under any law providing for preventive detention, the authority making the order shall, as soon as may be communicate to such person the grounds on which the order has been made, and shall afford the earliest opportunity of making a representation against the order:

Provided that the authority making any such order may refuse to disclose facts which such authority considers to be against the public interest to disclose.

Article 43: Protection of Home and Correspondence

Every citizen shall have the right, subject to any reasonable restrictions imposed by law in the interest of the security of the State, public order, public morality or public health–

(a) to be secured in his home against entry, search and seizure; and

(b) to the privacy of his correspondence and other means of communication.

APPENDIX–II

RELEVANT PROVISIONS OF THE FUNDAMENTALS OF THE CODE OF CRIMINAL PROCEDURE (CR. P. C.) IN BANGLADESH

Section 54: When Police May Arrest Without Warrant

Police Officer may, without an order from a Magistrate and without a warrant, arrest-

- *first of all,* any person who has been concerned in any cognisable offence or against whom a reasonable complaint has been made or credible information has been received, or a reasonable suspicion exists of his having been so concerned;
- *secondly,* any person having in his possession without lawful excuse, the burden of proving which excuse shall lie on such person, any implement of housebreaking;
- *thirdly,* any person who has been proclaimed as an offender either under this Code or by order of the Government;
- *fourthly,* any person in whose possession anything is found which may reasonable be suspected to be stolen property, and who may reasonable be suspected of having committed an offence with reference to such thing;
- *fifthly,* any person who obstructs a Police Officer while in the execution of his duty, or who has escaped, or attempts to escape, from lawful custody;
- *sixthly,* any person reasonably suspected of being a deserter from the armed forces of Bangladesh;
- *seventhly,* any person who has been concerned in, or against whom a reasonable complaint has been made or credible information has been received or a reasonable suspicion exists of his having been concerned in, any act committed in Bangladesh, would have been punishable as an offence, and for which he is, under any law relating to extradition or under the Fugitive Offenders Act 1881, or otherwise, liable to be apprehended or detained in custody in Bangladesh;
- *eighthly,* any released convict committing a breach of any rule made under Section 565, Sub-section (3);
- *ninthly,* any person for whose arrest a requisition has been received from another Police Officer, provided that the

requisition specified the person to be arrested and the offence or other cause for which the arrest is to be made and it appears therefrom that the person might lawfully be arrested without a warrant by the officer who issued the requisition.

Section 167: Procedure when Investigation Cannot be Completed in Twenty-four Hours

(1) Whenever any person is arrested and detained in custody, and it appears that the investigation cannot be completed within the period of twenty-four hours fixed by Section 61, and there are grounds for believing that the accusation or information is well-founded, the Officer-in-charge of the police station of the police Officer making the investigation if he is not below the rank of Sub-inspector shall forthwith transmit to the nearest Magistrate a copy of the entries in the diary hereinafter prescribed relating to the case, and shall at the same time forward the accused to such Magistrate.

(2) The Magistrate to whom an accused person is forwarded under this section may, whether he has or has not jurisdiction to try the case, from time to time, authorise the detention of the accused in such custody as such Magistrate thinks fit, for a term not exceeding fifteen days in the whole. If he has not jurisdiction to try the case or send it for trial, and considers further detention unnecessary, he may order the accused to be forwarded to a Magistrate having such jurisdiction.

Provided that no Magistrate of the third class, and no Magistrate of the second class not specially empowered in this behalf by the Government shall authorise detention in the custody of the police.

(3) A Magistrate authorising under this Section detention in the custody of the police shall record his reasons for so doing.

(4) If such order is given by a Magistrate other than the Chief Metropolitan Magistrate (CMM), District Magistrate (DM) or Sub-divisional Magistrate (SDM), he shall forward a copy of his order, with his reasons for making it, to the Magistrate to whom he is immediately sub-ordinate.

(5) If the investigation is not concluded within one hundred and twenty days from the date of receipt of the information relating to the commission of the offence or the order of the Magistrate for such investigation.

(a) the Magistrate empowered to take cognisance of such offence or making the order for investigation may, if the offence to which the investigation relates is not punishable with death, imprisonment for life or imprisonment exceeding ten years, release the accused on bail to the satisfaction of such Magistrate; and

(b) the Court of Session may, if the offence to which the investigation relates is punishable with death imprisonment for life or imprisonment exceeding ten years, release the accused on bail to the satisfaction of such court;

Provided that if an accused is not released on bail under this sub-section, the Magistrate or, as the case may be, the Court of Session shall record the reasons for it;

Provided further that in cases in which sanction of appropriate authority is required to be obtained under the provisions of the relevant law for prosecution of the accused, the time taken for obtaining such sanction shall be excluded from the period specified in this sub-section.

APPENDIX–III
RELEVANT PROVISIONS OF THE SPECIAL POWERS ACT, 1974 (SPA) IN BANGLADESH

Section 3: Power to Make Order Detaining or Removing Certain Persons

(2) Any District Magistrate or Additional District Magistrate may if satisfied with respect to any person that with a view to preventing him from doing any prejudicial act within the meaning of Section 2(f)(iii), (iv), (v), (vi), (vii), or (viii), it is necessary so to do, make an order directing that such person detained;

(3) When any order made is under Sub-section (2), the District Magistrate or Additional District Magistrate making the order shall forthwith report the fact to the Government. Together with the grounds on which the order has been made and such other particulars as, in his opinion, have a bearing on the matter, and no such order shall remain in force for more than thirty days after the making thereof unless in the meantime it has approved by the government.

Section 8: Communication of Grounds of Order

(1) In every case where an order has been made under Section 3, the authority making the order shall as soon as may be but subject to the provisions of Sub Section (2), communicate to the person affected thereby the grounds on which the order has been made enable him to make a representation in writing against the order, and it shall be the duty of such authority to inform such person of his right of making such representation and to afford him the earliest opportunity of doing so;

Provided that nothing in this Section shall require the authority to disclose the facts which it considers to be against the public interest to disclose.

(2) In the case of a detention order, the authority making the order shall inform the person detained under that order of the grounds of his detention at the time he is detained as soon thereafter as is practicable, but not later than fifteen days from the date of detention.

Section 10: Reference To Advisory Board

In every case where a detention order has been made under this Act, the Government shall, within one hundred and twenty days from the date of detention under the order, place before the Advisory Board constituted under Section 9 the ground on which the order has been made and the representation, if any, made by the person affected by the order.

Section 11: Procedure of Advisory Board

(1) The Advisory Board shall, after considering the materials placed before it and calling for such further information as it may deem necessary from the Government or from the person concerned and after affording the person concerned and opportunity of being heard in person, submit its report to the Government within one hundred and seventy days from the date of detention.

APPENDIX–IV
RELEVANT PROVISIONS OF THE UNIVERSAL DECLARATION OF HUMAN RIGHTS (UDHR)

Article 3

Every one has the right to life, liberty and the security of person.

Article 5

No one shall be subjected to torture or to cruel, inhuman or degrading treatment or punishment.

Article 9

No one shall be subjected to arbitrary arrest, detention or exile.

Article 10

Everyone is entitled in full equality to a fair trial and public hearing by an independent and impartial tribunal, in the determination of his rights and obligations and of criminal charge against him.

Article 11

1. Everyone charged with a penal offence has the right to be presumed innocent until proved guilty according to law in a public trial at which he has had all the guarantees necessary for his defence.
2. No one shall be held guilty of any penal offence on account of any act or omission, which did not constitute a penal offence, under national or international law, at the time when it was committed. Nor shall a heavier penalty be imposed than the one that was applicable at the time the penal offence was committed.

APPENDIX–V
RELEVANT PROVISIONS OF THE INTERNATIONAL COVENANT ON CIVIL AND POLITICAL RIGHTS (ICCPR)

Article 9: Liberty and Security of Person

1. Everyone has the right to liberty and security of person. No one shall be subjected to arbitrary arrest or detention. No one shall be deprived of his liberty except on such grounds and in accordance with such procedure as are established by law.
2. Anyone who is arrested shall be informed, at the time of arrest, of the reasons for his arrest and shall be promptly informed of any charges against him.
3. Anyone arrested or detained on a criminal charge shall be brought promptly before a judge or other officer authorised by law to exercise judicial power and shall be entitled to trial within a reasonable time or to release. It shall not be the general rule that persons awaiting trial shall be detained in custody, but release may be subject to guarantees to appear for trial, at any other stage of the judicial proceedings, and, should occasion arise, for execution of the judgement.
4. Anyone who is deprived of his liberty by arrest or detention shall be entitled to take proceedings before a court, in order that court may decide without delay on the lawfulness of his detention and order his release if the detention is not lawful.
5. Anyone who has been the victim of unlawful arrest or detention shall have an enforceable right to compensation.

Article 14: Procedural Guarantees in Criminal Trial

1. All persons shall be equal before the courts and tribunals. In the determination of any criminal charge against him, or of his rights and obligations in a suit at law, everyone shall be entitled to a fair and public hearing by a competent, independent and impartial tribunal established by law. The press and the public may be excluded from all or part of a trial for reasons of morals, public order or national security in a democratic society, or when the interest of the private lives of the parties so requires, or to the extent strictly necessary in the opinion of the court in special circumstances where publicity would prejudice the interests of justice; but any judgement rendered in a criminal case or in a suit at law shall be made public except where the interest of

juvenile persons otherwise requires or the proceedings concern matrimonial disputes or the guardianship of children.

2. Everyone charged with a criminal offence shall have the right to be presumed innocent until proved guilty according to law.

3. In the determination of any criminal charge against him, everyone shall be entitled to the following minimum guarantees, in full equality:

   (a) To be informed promptly and in detail in a language which he understands of the nature and cause of the charge against him;

   (b) To have adequate time and facilities for the preparation of his defence and to communicate with counsel of his own choosing;

   (c) To be tried without undue delay;

   (d) To be tried in his presence, and to defend himself in person or through legal assistance of his own choosing; to be informed, if he does not have legal assistance, of this right; and to have legal assistance, assigned to him, in any case where the interests of justice so require, and without payment by him in any such case if he does not have sufficient means to pay for it;

   (e) To examine, or have examined, the witness against him and to obtain the attendance and examination of witnesses on his behalf under the same conditions as witnesses against him;

   (f) To have the assistance of an interpreter if he cannot understand or speak the language used in court;

   (g) Not to be compelled to testify against himself or to confess guilt.

4. In the case of juvenile persons, the procedure shall be such as will take account of their age and the desirability of promoting their rehabilitation.

5. Everyone convicted of a crime shall have the right to his conviction and sentence being reviewed by a higher tribunal according to law.

6. When a person has by a final decision been convicted of a criminal offence and when subsequently his conviction has been reversed or he has been pardoned on the ground that a new or newly

discovered fact shows conclusively that there has been a miscarriage of justice, the person who has suffered punishment a s a result of such conviction shall be compensated according to law, unless it is proved that the non-disclosure of the unknown fact in time is wholly or partly attributable to him.

7. No one shall be liable to be tried or punished again for an offence for which ha has already been convicted or acquitted in accordance with the law and penal procedure of each country.

APPENDIX –VI
A LIST OF DRESS FOR THE WOMEN PRISONERS

Rule 1159 of the Bengal Jail Code

All prisoners in Division III sentenced to rigorous imprisonment shall be furnished, on admission, with the following jail equipment:

Female prisoners

2 cotton chemises or *kurtas*

10 yards of cotton cloth 42 inches wide

2 *gumchas*

1 blanket coat

1 *tatputtee* for bedding

2 blankets

1 aluminium cup

1 aluminium plate

A square (2ft.×2ft.) of coarse gunny or matting

1 comb

Rule 1165 of the Bengal Jail Code

Convicted prisoners in Division II sentenced to rigorous imprisonment shall be furnished with the following jail equipment:

(a) For the Hot Weather

Accustomed to European mode of living		Accustomed to Indian mode of living:	
Cotton skirts	2	Saries (pairs)	2
Cotton blouses	2	Cotton blouses	2
Cotton shirts	2	Chemise or shirts	2
Cotton drawers (pairs)	2	Drawers (pairs)	2
Cotton stockings (pairs)	2	Stockings (pairs)	2
Garters (pair)	1	Garters (pair)	1
Leather belt	1		
Cap	1		
Sola topi	1		

(b) For the Cold Weather and Rains

Accustomed to European mode of living		Accustomed to Indian mode of living:	
Cotton skirt	1	Saries (pairs)	3
Cotton blouse	1	Cotton blouse	1
Woollen shirt	1	Woollen blouse	1
Woollen blouse	1	Flannel shirts or chemise	2
Flannel shirts	2	Cotton drawers (pairs)	2
Cotton drawers (pairs)	2	Stockings (pairs)	2
Cotton stockings (pairs)	2	Garters (pair)	1
Leather belt	1		
Garters (pair)	1		
Cap	1		
Sola topi	1		

BIBLIOGRAPHY

LEGISLATION

Bengal Jail Code 1894 (Bangladesh).

Bill of Rights 1689 (England).

Code of Civil Procedure 1908 (As amended up to 2000).

Code of Criminal Procedure 1898 (Bangladesh).

Constitution of Bangladesh 1972 (As amended up to 2000).

Constitution of India 1950 (As amended up to 2000).

Constitution of Pakistan 1956 (As amended up to 2000).

Penal Code 1860 (Bangladesh).

Special Powers Act 1974 (Bangladesh).

The Evidence Act 1872 (Bangladesh).

The Prisoners Act 1900 (As amended up to 2000).

The Prisons Act 1894 (As amended up to 2000).

INTERNATIONAL INSTRUMENTS

Charter of United Nations 1945.

Optional Protocol to the International Covenant on Civil and Political Rights 1966.

Universal Declaration of Human Rights 1948.

UN Declaration on the Right to Development 1986.

REGIONAL INSTRUMENTS

African Charter on Human and Peoples' Rights 1981.

American Convention on Human Rights 1969.

Arab Charter on Human Rights 1994.

European Convention for the Protection of Human Rights and Fundamental Freedoms 1950.

CASES

Abdul Gani vs. State, 16 DLR 388.

Abdul Mannan vs. The State, 14 DLR 667.

Abdur Rahman vs. State, 29 DLR 256 (SC).

Acosta vs. Uruguay, Thirty-ninth Session (A/39/40), annex. XI.

Ajmer Sign vs. S.P. SCR (1953) 418.

Ajor Ali Sarder vs. The State, 41 DLR 306.

Ataur Rahman vs. The State, 42 DLR 31, AD.

Australia vs. Italy, Yearbook VI (1963), 740.

Babu Khan vs. State, 55 DLR 547.

Bilkis Akhtar Hossain vs. Bangladesh, 2 MLR (1997).

BLAST vs. Bangladesh, 55 DLR (2003) 363.

Bolanos vs. Ecuador, Forty-fourth session (A/44/40), annex XIX.

Bolanos vs. Ecuador, No. 238/1987, SS. 2.1. 8.3.9.

Bombay vs. Kathi Kalu, AIR 1961 SC 1808.

Caldas vs. Uruguay, Report of the Human Rights Committee, Official Records of the General Assembly, *Forty-fifth Session* (A/45/40), Vol. II, annex IX. K.

Conteris vs. Uruguay, Report of the Forty-first session (A/41/40), annex VIII C, Para. 1.5.

Counselman vs. Hitchcock, 142 US 547.

DBM Patnaik vs. State of AP, AIR 1971 SC 2092.

DK Basu vs. State of West Bengal, AIR (Sec) 610, 1997.

Farzana Huq vs. Bangladesh, 43 DLR (1991) 501.

Fazar Ali vs. Sikander Ali, 44 DLR (1992) 49.

Frank vs. Delawse, 98 SC 2674, 1978.

Gilboa vs. Uruguay, Forty-first session (A/41/40), annex VIII.B.

Golam A Maula vs. The State, 46 DLR 140.

Gomez de Voituret vs. Uruguay, Report of the Forty-first session (A/41/40), annex VIII C.

H M Ershad vs. Bangladesh, 52 DLR (AD) 162.

Habiba Mahmud vs. Bangladesh, 45 DLR (AD) (1993) 89.

Hoslide vs. Crown, 44 CWN 82.

Hussainara Kahtoon vs. State of Bihar, AIR 1979, SC 1360.

Hussainara Khatoon, AIR 1979 SC 1819.

Karak Sing vs. MP, AIR 1963 SC 1295.

Kelly vs. Jamaica (1997) 4 IHRR 334.

Lafuente Penarrieta et al. vs. Bolivia, Communication No. *176/1984 (CCPR/C/OP/2), 1990.*

Lafuente Penarrieta et al. vs. Bolivia, Vol. II, Communication No. 176/1984 (CCPR/C/OP/2), 1990.

Lawrence vs. The King, (1933), AC 699.

Le Compte, van Leuven and De Meyere Case, Report of 14 December 1979 paras. 90-91.

Maharashtra vs. Champalal, AIR 1981 SC 1675.

Malakani vs. Maharastra, AIR 1973 SC 157.

Mashall vs. Barlours, 98 SC 1816.

Md Sekandar Ali vs. Bangladesh, 42 DLR 346.

Mehnaz Sakib vs. Bangladesh, 52 DLR (HD) 526.

Minanda vs. Arizona, 348 US 436.

Mobarak Ali (Md.) alias Mobarak Ali Mondal vs. People's Republic of Bangladesh (represented by the Ministry of Home Affairs), 50 DLR 10.

Mohammad Siddiqur Rehman vs. State, 7 BLD 93 (AD).

Mokbul Hossain vs. Government of Bangladesh and Others, 54 DLR 118.

Montejo vs. Colombia, Report of Thirty-seventh Session (A/37/40), annex XV.

Morael vs. France, Communication No. 207/1986, para. 9.3.

MP Sharma vs. Satish Chandra, 1077 SCR (1954) 1088.

Munoz Hermoza vs. Peru, Communication No. 203/1986, para. 11.3, 12.

Nandini vs. Satiapathy, (1978) SCC CN 236.

Narayanlal and *Dastagir,* AIR 1961 SC 29; AIR 1960 SC 756.

Nasima Begum vs. Bangladesh, 49 DLR (AD) (1997) 102.

Nasrin Kader Siddiqui vs. Bangladesh, 44 DLR (AD) (1992) 16.

Pett vs. Greyhound Racing Assn, 2 All ER (1968) 545.

Pinto vs. Trinidad and Tobago, Report of the Forty-fifth Session (A/45/40), Vol. II. annex IX H.

Prabhakar Pandurag vs. State of Makarastra, AIR 1966 SC 424.

Pratt and Morgan vs. Jamaica, Forty-fourth Session (A/44/40), annex X.F.

Reita Rahman vs. Bangladesh, 50 DLR (1998) 201.

Saifuzzaman vs. State, 56 DLR (2004) 324.

Sanjay Suri vs. Delhi Administration, CrLJ (1988) 705 (SC).

Sheela Barse vs. State of Maharastra, AIR 1983 SC 378.

Silrerthorne Lamber Co. vs. US, 251 US 385.

Silrerthorne Lamber Co. vs. US, 251 US 385.

Silverman v. US, 365 US 505.

State of Maharashtra vs. Champalal, 25 JILI (1983) 90.

State of UP vs. Deoman Upadhyaya, AIR (1960) SC 1125.

State vs. Robiul Hossain alias Rob, 52 DLR (HCD) 370.

Sunil Batra vs. Delhi Administration, AIR 1978 SC 1675.

The Crown vs. Adalat, 8 DLR 69, FC.

The State vs. Abdul Gazi, 33 DLR 79.

The State vs. Imdad Ali Bepary, 36 DLR 333.

Van Alphen vs. The Netherlands, Report of the Forty-fifth Session (A/45/40), Vol.II. annex. IX M.

VMRB vs. Canada, No. 236/1987.

Weeks vs. US, 232 US 383.

Wight vs. Madagascar, (1985) 2 Selected Decisions of HRC 151 at 154.

X v. Austria, D & R 18 (1980), 160 and Appeal No. 8289/78.

X v. Belgium, D & R 16 (1979), 200 and Appeal No. 8417/78.

X vs. FRG, D & R 17 (1980), 231 and Appeal No. 8417/78.

X vs. Sweden, Yearbook II (1958-1959), 354 and Appeal No. 434/58.

Zand Case, D & R 15 (1979), 70.

Zilaluddin vs. Bangladesh, 54 DLR (2002) 625.

SECONDARY SOURCES

Books

Ahmad S. M. (2003), *Police Regulations of Bengal* 1943, Dhaka.

Alston P. (Ed.) (1995) *Promoting Human Rights through Bills of Rights: Comparative Perspectives*, Oxford: Clarendon Press.

Alston P, (Ed.) (1992), *The United Nations and Human Rights: A Critical Appraisal*, Oxford: Clarendon Press, New York; Oxford University Press.

Bassiouni M. and Cherif (Ed.) (1994), *The Protection of Human Rights in the Administration of Criminal Justice: A Compendium of United Nations Norms and Standards*, Transnational Publishers.

Batra M. (1989), *Protection of Human Rights in Criminal Justice Administration*, New Delhi, Deep & Deep Publications.

Beatty D M. (1994), *Human Rights and Judicial Review: A Comparative Perspective*, Martinus Nijhoff Publishers, London.

Bhuian M. N. (2002), *Protection of Human Rights at the International Level: Effectiveness of the Human Rights Committee and the 1503 Procedure*, AIUB, Dhaka.

Black's Law Dictionary 4th Ed.

BLD'S 8-Years Criminal Digest 1993-2000 (2002), Bangladesh Bar Council, Dhaka.

Bossuyt M. J. (1987), *Guide to the Travaux Preparatories of the International Covenant on Civil and Political Rights*, Dordrecht: Martinus Nijhoff Publishers.

Brownlie (1972), *Basic Documents in International Law*, Oxford.

Buergental T. (1996), *International Human Rights*, Washington DC.

Cassese A. (1990), *Human Rights in a Changing World*, Philadelphia: Temple University Press.

Centre for Human Rights (1995), *United Nations action in the Field of Human Rights,* New York: United Nations.

Chaturveeli A. N. (1984), *Rights of Accused under Indian Constitution,* Deep & Deep Publications, New Delhi.

Cook J. G. (1972), *Constitutional Rights of the Accused, Pre-trial Rights,* (The Lawyers Co-operative Publishing Co., Rochester, New York:).

Cook R. (Ed.) (1994), *Human Rights of Women: National and International Perspectives,* Philadelphia: University of Pennsylvania Press.

Corretta P., Cox G. and Pease K., *World Factbook of Criminal Justice System: England and Wales.*

Crawford J. (ed.) (1992), *The Rights of Peoples,* Oxford: Clarendon Press; New York: Oxford University Press.

Dijk P van and Hoof GJH van (1983) *Theory and practice of the European Convention,* (Kluwer Deventer Publishers

Dijk P. V. (1983), *The Right of Accused to a Fair trial under International Law,* Utrecht.

Dijk P. V. and Hoof G. J. H. V. (1983), *Theory and practice of the European Convention,* Kluwer Deventer Publishers.

Dijk P. V. and Hoof G. J. H. V. (1990), *Theory and Practice of the European Convention on Human Rights,* 2nd ed., Deventer; Boston: Kluwer Law and Taxation Publishers.

Donnelly J. (1993), *International Human Rights,* Boulder, CO: Westview Press.

Donnelly J. (1985), *The Concept of Human Rights,* New York: St. Martin's Press.

Donnelly J. (1989), *Universal Human Rights in Theory and Practice,* Ithaca, NY: Cornell University Press.

English K. and Stapleton A. (1997), *The Human Rights Handbook: A Practical Guide to Monitoring Human Rights,* Juta & Co. Ltd.

Fellman D. (1966), *The Defendant's Rights under English Law,* Madison: Wisconsin U. P.

Fitzpatrick J. (1994), *Human Rights in Crisis: The International System for Protecting Human Rights During States of Emergency,* Philadelphia: University of Pennsylvania Press.

Francis JG (1975) *The European Convention on Human Rights,* Oxford.

Ghandhi P. R. (Ed.) (2000), *Blackstone's International Human Rights Documents*, 2nd Edition, Blackstone Press Limited, London

Gibbons D. C. (1978), *Society, Crime and Criminal Career*, Prentice Hall of India, Delhi.

Gross H. (1962), *Criminal Investigation*, (Fifth Edition, Sweet & Maxwell Ltd.).

Harris D. J. (1998), *Cases and Materials on International Law*, Sweet & Maxwell, London.

Henkin L. (Ed.) (1981), *The International Bill of Rights: The Covenant on Civil and Political Rights*, New York: Columbia University Press.

Hertzberg S. and Zammuto C. (1981), *The Protection of Human Rights in the Criminal Process under International Instruments and National Constitutions*, Sicily.

Hertzberg S. and Zammuto C. (1981), *The Protection of Human Rights in the Criminal Process under International Instruments and National Constitutions*, Sicily.

Hobbs T. (1914), *Leviathan*, Aldinepress, Letchworth.

Human Rights in Bangladesh: A study of Standards and Practices, BILIA Publication, Dhaka.

Huq M. E. (2001), *Criminal Justice System Administration*, (Ahsania Mission, Dhaka).

Huq Z. (2001), *Law and Practice of Criminal Procedure*, Bangladesh Law Book Company, Dhaka.

Islam M. (1995), *Constitutional Law of Bangladesh*, (4th Edition, BILIA Publication, Dhaka).

Islam M. Z. (1989), *The Code of Criminal Procedure*, Enayet Murshida Islam, Chuadanga (Bangladesh).

Kalaiah A. B. (1986), *Human Rights in International Law*, New Delhi.

Kelkar R. V. (1984), *Outlines of Criminal Procedure*, Deep & Deep Publications, New Delhi.

Kibria ABMG (1976), *Police Administration in Bangladesh*, (First Edition, Jatya mudarn).

Lauterpatch (1968), *International Law and Human Rights*, U.S.A.

Legal Remembrance's Manual 1960.

Mayer A. (1991) *Islam and Human Rights: Tradition and Politics*, Boulder, CO: Westview Press.

McGoldrick D. (1994), *The Human Rights Committee: Its Role in the Development of the International Covenant on Civil and Political Rights,* Oxford University Press, Clarendon Press, New York.

Meron T. (Ed.) (1984), *Human Rights in International Law: Legal and Policy Issues,* Oxford: Clarendon Press.

Nowak M. (1993), *UN Covenant on Civil and Political Rights: CCPR Commentary,* Kehl: Engel Publishers.

Rane D. and Khanna S.L., *Comparative Law (History of Common Law),* Oriental Publishers.

Report of the Human Rights Committee, Official Records of the General Assembly, Forty-fifth Session (A/45/40), Vol. II, annex IX K.

Robertson A. H. (1999), *Human Rights in the World,* Manchester University Press.

Salmond W .G . (1985), *Jurisprudence,* (12th Edition, Maxwell).

Sarker A. H. (2005), *Criminology: Theory and Analysis,* Kollol Prokashony, Dhaka.

Seighart P. (1984), *The International Law of Human Rights,* Oxford.

Sharma P. D. (1985), *Police and Criminal Justice Administration in India.*

Stephen J. F. (1883), *A History of Criminal Law in England,* London.

Stephen J. F. (1883), *A History of Criminal Law of England,* London.

Thakker C. K. (1956), *Administrative Law,* (1st Edition, Eastern Book Company, Lalbagh, Lucknow).

Ud-Din M. F. (1999), *Ayeen: Probandha Sankalon,* Rajshahi (Bangladesh).

Ud-Din M. F. and Hannan M. A. (2000), 'Protection of Human Rights in Criminal Justice: Bangladesh Perspective', *Research Project* 1998, Rajshahi University, Bangladesh.

Zamir Muhammad (1990), *Human Rights Issues and International Law,* University Press, Dhaka.

Articles

Bari M. E., 'The Universal Declaration of Human Rights ‾The *Magna Carta* of Mankind', *Human Rights and Development Review,* Vol. V, (1995), Humanist and Ethical Association of Bangladesh, Dhaka.

Baxi U. (1983), 'Right to Speedy Trial geare, gander and Judicial Sauce (*State of Maharashtra vs. Champalal*)', 25 Indian Journal of International Law 90 at 105.

Bhagwati P. N. (1986), 'Human Rights in the Criminal Justice', *12 Indian Bar Review*, 22.

Brody (1991), 'The United Nations Creates a Working Group on Arbitrary Detention, *American Journal of International Law*, 709.

Haque E. (1997), 'Criminal Justice Administration Prerequisite for Security and Freedom', *Human Rights Law*, (Dhaka).

Haque M. J. (1997), 'Human Rights and Right to Liberty: Before and Now', *Human Rights Law*, Dhaka.

Hasan J. and Hussain S. (2004), 'Human Rights and Police Custody: A Perspective of Dhaka Metropolitan Police', *The Bangladesh Today*, Dhaka (Bangladesh), 7 August.

Hossain KUJ, 'The International Bill of Human Rights and Bangladesh', *Human Rights Law*, Dhaka: 1997

Husain M. (2000), 'Effective Criminal Procedure and Judicial Strength', *The Independent*, Dhaka, 14 August.

Kabir A. H. M. (1998), 'Policing the Police', *The Daily Star*, Dhaka (Bangladesh) 2 August.

Khan A. R. (2000), 'State of Human Rights: National Security Laws in Bangladesh', *The Daily Star*, Dhaka (Bangladesh), 30 January.

Khan H. (1993), 'The Role of Judiciary in the Promotion and Protection of Human Rights', *The Dhaka University Studies (Part F)*, Vol. IV, June.

Nigam K. K. (1962), 'Due Process of Law: A Comparative Study of Procedural Guarantees Against Deprivation of Personal Liberty in the United States and India', *4 Indian Journal of International Law*, 99

Patwary M. I., 'Human Rights in Islamic Law and Modern International Law: A Comparative Study', *Human Rights and Development Review*, Vol. V, (1995), Humanist and Ethical Association of Bangladesh Publications.

Rahman, A.M.M.J. (1966), 'Human Rights and the Role of Judiciary', *The Main Stream Law Reports*, Vol. 1, Dhaka.

Rahman, A.M.M.J. (1997), 'Human Rights Violation and Remedies under Constitutional Law of Bangladesh', *The Main Stream Law Reports*, Vol. 11, Dhaka.

Ud-Din M.F., 'Human Rights and Constitutional Guarantees: Bangladesh Perspective', *The Islamic University Studies*, (Vol. 2 No. 1, 2000), Faculty of Law, Islamic University, Kushtia.

Ud-Din M.F., 'The Protection and Promotion of Human Rights: International Perspective', *Law Journal of the Faculty of Law* 1998, Rajshahi University, Bangladesh.

JOURNALS ON HUMAN RIGHTS

Australian Human Rights Booklets, Australian Human Rights Information Centre, 1995.

Canadian Human Rights Yearbook, Toronto: Carswell, 1983.

Chittagong University Journal of Law, Chittagong, Vol. V, 2000.

Columbia Human Rights Law Review, New York: Columbia University School of Law, 1972.

Harvard Human Rights Journal, Cambridge, MA: Harvard Law School, 1988.

Human Rights Law Journal, Kehl am Rhein: NP Engel, 1980.

Netherlands Quarterly of Human Rights, Utrecht: Studie-en Informatiecntrum Mesenrechten, 1983.

South African Journal on Human Rights, Johnnesburg: Centre for Applied Legal Studies, University of Witwatersrand, 1985.

Journal of the Institute of Bangladesh Studies, Rajshahi University, Bangladesh, Vol. 27, 2004 .

REPORTS ON HUMAN RIGHTS

Annual Report 2002 of the BRCT, Dhaka.

Annual Report 2003 of the BRCT, Dhaka.

Human Rights Fact-Finder, (BRCT, Dhaka: March-April, 1997).

Human Rights Today-UN Briefing Papers, (UN Publications: October, 1998).

Law Commission of Bangladesh, Annual Report (1997), Vol. II (Bangladesh).

INDEX

A

Abdul Gani Vs State, 29

Abdul Mannan Vs State, 29

Abdur Rahman Vs State, 30

Abus Saffar Case, 45

Academy for Educational Development, 42

Administration, 100

  Autocratic, 85

  Criminal Justice-, 78

  Of Criminal Justice, 7

  Of Justice, 4, 100, 102, 126

Advisory Board, 33-35, 71

Afghanistan, 177

African Charter on Human and Peoples, (ACHPR), 21, 42

Ain'o Shalish Kendra, 9

Alamgir Kabir of Nowgaon, 19

Alauddin Khan, 26

Algeria, 177

American

  Convention on Human Rights, (ACHR), 21, 42, 130, 139

  Declaration of the Rights and Duties of Man, 21, 41

  Supreme Court, 40

Amnesty International Report Features, 81, 82

ANSAR, 4, 21, 22, 44, , 133, 134

Anti-Humanitarian Law, 69

Arbitrary Arrest and Detention, 61

Armed Forces of Bangladesh, 23

Awami League, 74

B

Babu Khan, 26

Bail, As matter of Right, 68

Bailable Offences, 68

Bangladesh, 3, 5, 7-11, 17, 18, 20, 23, 24, 40, 56, 77, 79, 80, 82, 83, 85, 94, 101,102, 107, 111-113, 116, 117, 132, 133, 134, 141, 154-158, 166, 178

  Administration of Justice in-, 10

  Constitution Law of-, 13

  Constitution of-, 4-6, 18, 19, 20 see under Constitution also

Crime Situation in-, 4
Criminal Justice of-, 11
Criminal Justice Administration in-, 8
Criminal Laws of-, 63
Criminal Legislation of-, 101
Criminals in-, 7
Female Prisoners of-, 154
Human Rights Bureau (BHRB), 80
Human Rights in-, 19, 61, 81, 181
Law Enforcement Agencies, (LEA), 23
Law Making Body of-, 178
Laws and Practices, 8
Laws of-, 5, 7, 178
LEA in Bangladesh, 78
Legal Aid and Services Trust (BLAST), 9
Life and Property in-, 7
Military Rule, 9
Modern Prisons of-, 136
Municipal Law of-, 3, 4
National Party (BNP), 71, 74
Police, 85, 88
Police Administration in-, 12
Political Opposition Leaders, 140
Rifles (BDR), 4, 21, 22, 44, 133, 134
Role of Police in -, 78
State of Human Rights in-, 166
Supreme Court of-, 67

Basic Human Rights, 3, 5, 74
Bengal Jail Code, 153
Blast Case, 25, 36, 46, 51, 53, 56
Blast Vs Bangladesh, 46, 82
BMSP (Bangladesh Manobidikar Shamannoy Parishad), 9
Bolivian, 64
Bombs, 19
Bosnia, 177
BRCT, Bangladesh Rehabilitation Centre for Trauma Victims, (BRCT), 9, 45, 80, 141, 147
Fact Finding Team, 153
Report, 22
British
Administration, 141
Criminal Administration of Justice, 107
Prison Model, 136
Rule, 139

C

Capacity of Prisons in Bangladesh, 142
Capital Punishment, 21
Cases under Special Police Power Act, 72
Chittagong
Medical College Hospital, 44
Metropolitan Police Act, 51
Chowdhury, Abdur Rahman, Justice, 71
Code of Criminal Procedure, 5

Relevant Provisions, 187-189

Committee of Experts of Council of Europe, 65

Common Law System, 12

Constitution of Bangladesh, 22, 31, 38, 40, 42, 54, 63, 67-69, 77, 83, 109, 111-103, 116, 127, 128, 132, 134, 135, 178

Relevant Provisions, 185-186

Constitution of

India, 21, 28

Pakistan, 21, 42

USA, 111, 113

Constitutional Guarantee, 41, 133

Convention Against Torture and Other—, 42

Corruption of Police, 85

Covert and Correctional System, 12

Crimes,

Control of-, 5, 6

Trends of-, 6

Criminal

Administration of Justice, 3

In Bangladesh, 101

Charges, 123

Investigation, 13, 102

Jurisprudence (tial), 111

Philosophy, 178

Principle, 63

Administration, 11, 12, 128

Administration System, 102, 106

Justice, (CJ), 1, 62, 66, 100

Administration of-, 2

Justice System (CJS), 1, 2

Administration, 12

System, 10, 61, 100, 106, 112, 122

Law, 1, 2, 102

Legislation, 100-102, 178

Legislation, In Bangladesh, 104

Penal Code, 23, 24, 27-30, 39, 46-49, 52, 53, 64, 66, 71, 76, 77, 82, 83, 88-91, 93, 104, 105, 108, 110, 112, 116, 126, 166, 169, 171, 175, 179, 180

Prosecutions, 64

Criminals, 20

Custodial

Deaths, 22, 79

Torture, 149

D

Declaration on the Right to Development, 190

Degrading Treatment, 133, 134, 136, 138

Deprivation of Liberty, 62, 66, 67

Detention, 69

Types, 69

Preventive, 69

Punitive, 69, 70

Developing Countries, 67

Dhaka

Central Jail, 146, 148

Metropolitan Police Ordinance, 134

District
    Jessore, 20
    Police Stations, (DPS), 166
        Barishal, 166
        Chhittagon, 166
        Comila, 166
        Dhaka, 166
        Faridpur, 166
        Jessore, 166
        Jhenaidah, 166
    Rajshahi, 166
DK Basu Vs State of West Bengal, 91
Drug Offences, 12

E

Education of Minors, 62
England and Wales, 107
Ethical Values, 107
European Convention on Human Rights and Fundamental Freedoms, (ECHR), 21, 41, 65, 139
Evidence Act, 66, 111, 113
Evidence Act of US, 113

F

Fair
    Hearing, 124
    Trial, 122, 123, 135
Farzana Huq Vs Bangladesh, 73
Fetter Prisoners, 137
Foreign Prisoners, 141
French and Spanish, 65
Fugitive Offenders Act, 24
Fundamental
    Human Rights, 6, 18, 78, 135, 157, 178
    Principles of State Policy, 4
    Rights, 4-6, 17, 18, 51, 63, 69, 128, 149, 150

G

Gang Rape, 134
Gazi Muhammad Shahjahan, MP, Bangladesh, 71
General Assembly of UN, 133
Grenade Act, 40
Guardianship of Children, 126

H

Habib Mahmud Vs Bangladesh, 73
High Court Division Recommendations, 47-48
HM Ershad Vs Bangladesh, 115
Human Rights
    Commission, 8, 62, 64, 65, 67, 68, 124, 125, 127, 130, 131, 132
    Laws, 2
    Of Arrested/Detained Person, 61
    Organizations, 8
    Protection of-, 1
    Protection and Promotion of-, 181, 182
    Violation, 176, 177
Hussainara Case, 128

I

Illegal Detention, 166

Impartial Tribunals, 123

India and Pakistan, 4, 10

Indian

- Constitution, 127
- Criminal Justice System, 12
- Supreme Court, 111, 114

Inhuman/Degraded Treatment, 42

Institution Protection of Human Rights, 54

International

- Bill of Human Rights, 132
- Community, 3
- Covenant on Civil and Political Rights (ICCPR), 2, 8-10, 21, 41, 62-68, 93, 112, 122-124, 126, 127, 129-133, 136, 138, 139, 179, 180
  - Relevant Provisions, 193-195
- Covenant on Human Rights (ICHR), 2
- Human Rights, 2
- Human Rights Law, 122
- Police Cooperation (INTERPOL), 83, 84

Interview with

- Judicial Officers, 173
- Lawyers, 171
- Police Officers, 174
- Victims, 171

Ishral Ali, 170

J

Jail

- Code, 136, 140, 141, 145, 148, 149, 155, 157, 158
  - of Bangladesh, 152, 153
- Custody, 7, 22, 134, 166
- Management, 145
- Situation in Bangladesh, 122

Jessore Sub Jail, 20

Judicial

- Relief, 71
- Tribunals, 123

K

Kalim Gazi Shahpur Case, 45

Khalid Zia Regime, 9

Khulna Metropolitan Police Act, 51

Kosovo, 177

Kuldeep Singh, Justice, 90

L

Labour Union Activists, 6

Law (s)

- Enforcement, 3
- International, 7
- National and International, 5
- of Bangladesh, 66
- of Japan, 8
- of Russia, 8

LEA (Law Enforcement Agencies), 4, 5, 11, 18, 21, 22, 40, 42, 45, 61, 101, 118, 132, 134, 147, 153,, 166, 167, 172, 175, 178, 179, 181

Raping Women, 154

Legal

Custody, 129

Remembrance Manual (LRM), 26

System, 2, 5

M

M. Shah Nawaz Titu, 42, 43

Torture to Death, 42

Major Legal Systems, 8

India and Pakistan, 8

UK, 8

USA, 8

Md. Hamidul Haque, Justice, 25

Mehnaz Sakih Vs, Bangladesh, 30

MH Hannan, 170

Military Tribunal, 125

Ministry of Home Affairs, 88

Mirande Vs Arizona, 40

Mokbul Hossain Vs Bangladesh, 36

Mujibur Rahman, 19

Multinational Terrorism, 12

Munoz Hermoza Vs Peru, 124

Muslim Countries, 133

N

Nasim Begum Vs Bangladesh, 73

National

Conference on Human Rights, 22, 83

Human Rights Commission (NHRC), 54, 90

Human Rights Instruments (NHRI), 54

Independent Human Rights Commission, 56

Non-Bailable Offences, 68

Non-Cognizable Offences, 105

O & P

ODHIKAR, 42, 43

Pakistan, 134

Palestine, 177

Penal/Criminal Codes, 68

Police

Act, 1861, 42, 78

Code of Conduct, 90

Regulation Act, 115

Regulation of Bengal (PRB), 12, 84

Station Jails, 141

Pre-Trial Detention, 65, 67

Prevention Detention, 31, 68-70

Law, 36, 37

Under Special Power Act, 68

Principles of

Fair Deal, 124

Habeas Corpus, 66

Openess of Court, 126

Prison

Act of 1894, 1871, 1900, 136

Conditions, 135

In Bangladesh, 140

Crimes, 152

Reform Committee, 145

Prisoners and Their Types, 144
  Convicted Prisoners, 144
  Criminal Prisoners, 144
Prisoners,
  Criminal, 145
  Rights, 122
Prisons,
  Number in Banglaldesh, 141
  Overcrowding/Unhygienic, 141
  Types, 140
  In Bangladesh, 140
    Central Jails, 140
    District Jails, 140
    Subsidiary Jails, 141
    Thana Jails, 141
Prosecution and Defence, 124

R

RAB (Rapid Action Battalion), 21, 42, 43, 87, 88
Rajshahi
  Central Jail, 144
  Metropolitan Police Act, 51
  University, 170
Ram Pal, Justice, 151
Rape in Police Custody, 154
Right to
  An Appeal, 129
  Bail, 68
  Communicate on Grounds of Detention, 32
  Consult Lawyer, 28
  Fair Trial, 122
  Freedom from Torture—, 41
  Life and Liberty, 131
  Public Trial, 125
  Remedies/Compensation, 130
  Representation, 32
  Silence, 38, 108, 110, 111
  Speedy Trial, 126
Rights, 1
  Civil, 1, 17
  Cultural, 1, 17
  Economic, 1, 17
  Political, 1, 17
  Social, 1, 17
Role of Police, 61
  Accused Person, 61
  In Bangladesh, 61

S

Saipizaman Vs State, 51, 56
Sarwar Kamal, 170
Science and Technology, 11
Search/Seizure, 63
Search and Seizure of Accused Women, 117, 118
Security Measures, 66
Sentencing, 131
Sexual Abuse, 158
Shamim Raza Rubel Case, 46
Sheema Choudhury Case, 44
  Of Chittagong, 79
  Gang Raped Victim, 79, 134, 153

Garment Worker, 44
Sheikh Hasina Regime, 9
Silverman Vs US, 116
Social Security, 126
Socialist Law, 12
Society, 1, 3
Democratic, 123, 125
Just and Democratic-, 17
Soviet
Criminal Justice System, 12
Legal System, 12
Special Power Act (SPA), 1974, 6, 32-37, 61, 64, 66, 69-76, 90, 94, 166-168, 171, 173, 179, 180
Relevant Provisions, 190, 191
Special Rights for Persons in Custody, 64
Speedy Trial Tribunal Act, 128
Standard Minimum Rules for Treatment of Prisoners, 139
State of Maharashtra Vs Champalal, 127
State Vs Abdul Gazi, 28
State Vs Rahiul Hossain, 29
Supreme Court of Bangladesh, 111

T

Technical and Communicational Development, 83
Terrorist, 79
Torture
In Jail Custody, 147
Under Police Custody, 79
Trans-Border Human Trafficking, 12
Transparency International, 85
Trial Observers, 123
Tribunals, 128

U

UK and USA, 112
United Nations, (UN), 5, 62, 176
Demands, 62
Development Programmes, 54
Draft Body—, 2
General Assembly, 3, 180
Human Rights Committees, 8
Mission in Kampuchea, 83, 84
Mission in Yugoslavia, 84
Standard Minimum Rules for Treatment of Prisoners, 2
Transition Assistance Group (UNTAG), 84
Universal Declaration of Human Rights (UDHR), 2, 5, 9, 18, 41, 63, 122, 131-133, 157
Relevant Provisions, 192
Unlawful
Investigation, 63
Search and Seizure of Property, 114, 117
US, 10, 101, 112, 117
US Ambassador to Bangladesh, 102

V

Victims of Violence of Human Rights, 166

Violence

And Rights of the Accused, 46

Of Fundamental Rights, 40

Of Human Rights, 5, 6, 22, 61, 62, 79, 82, 166

Of Human Rights in Bangladesh, 172

W

Women Accused, 54

Constitutional Guarantee, 54

Women Prisoners, 153, 154, 157

Dress, 196-197

In Bangladesh, 153

Y & Z

Yoga, 152

Zilaluddin Vs Bangladesh, 35